General Educational Development Testing Ser...
A Program of the American Council on Educa...

Dear GED Candidate:

Congratulations on taking one of the most important steps of your life—earning a GED credential!

Since 1942, millions of people like you have taken the GED Tests to continue their education, to get a better job, or to achieve a sense of accomplishment.

We are delighted to introduce **Keys to GED® Success: Mathematics**—an invaluable resource to help you pass the GED Mathematics Test. It has been developed through a partnership between the GED Testing Service®—developer of the GED Tests—and Steck-Vaughn, a leading provider of GED test preparation materials and the exclusive distributor of the Official GED Practice Tests.

GEDTS researched the types of skills that GED candidates could focus on to improve their chances of passing the tests. We identified the types of questions and possible reasons that test-takers were missing specific questions on each test and decided to share that information. GEDTS collaborated with Steck-Vaughn to target those skills in a workbook that would benefit present and future GED candidates. The skills targeted in our research are called the **GED® Key Skills**—which is what you'll find in this book. In addition to the **GED Key Skills**, this book includes other important lessons that are needed to pass the GED Mathematics Test.

To help GED teachers, there is a Teaching Tips section included. The tips are written to address teaching strategies for some of the key problem areas that emerged from our research.

As the owner of this book, you can use the Pretest to determine exactly which skills you need to target to pass the test. Once you have completed your study, you can determine whether you are ready to take the GED Mathematics Test by taking an Official GED Practice Test—which follows Lesson 20. The GED Testing Service has developed this practice test as a predictor of the score that you will likely earn on the actual GED Mathematics Test.

Remember that there are four other books in the **Keys to GED Success** series. These other books cover the remaining four GED Tests: Language Arts, Reading, Science, Social Studies, and Language Arts, Writing. All titles in this series are available exclusively from Steck-Vaughn.

We wish you the best of luck on the GED Tests.

Executive Director
GED® Testing Service

September 2008

STECK-VAUGHN

Keys to GED® SUCCESS

Mathematics

Steck Vaughn™

HOUGHTON MIFFLIN HARCOURT
Supplemental Publishers

www.SteckVaughn.com/AdultEd
800-531-5015

ISBN-10:   1-4190-5347-7
ISBN-13: 978-1-4190-5347-4

3 4 5 6 7 8 9 1429 15 14 13 12 11 10

[Contents]

KEY **This symbol indicates** *GED* **®** *Key Skills* **as identified by the GED Testing Service®.**

[Using This Book]

Keys to GED® Success: Mathematics has been prepared by Steck-Vaughn in cooperation with the GED Testing Service®. This book focuses on the thinking and graphic interpretation skills needed to pass the GED Mathematics Tests.

This book also identifies the **GED® Key Skills**, which are skills that the GED Testing Service® has pinpointed as those most often missed by test takers who come close to passing the GED Tests. For more information about these skills see *A Message from the GED Testing Service®* at the front of this book.

In this book, the **GED Key Skills** are identified by this symbol: `KEY`

It is recommended that students who are preparing to take the GED Tests follow this plan:

1. Take the Mathematics Pretest.
While it is best to work through all the lessons in this book, students can choose to focus on specific skills. The *Mathematics Pretest* assesses the 20 skills in this book. The *Pretest Performance Analysis Chart* on page 9 will help students to target the skills that need the most attention.

2. Work through the 4-page skill lessons in the book.
- The first page of each lesson provides an approach to the skill and to thinking through the questions. Students should carefully read the step-by-step thinking strategies and pay attention to the explanations of why the correct answers are right and why the wrong answer choices are incorrect.

- The second page of each lesson contains sample GED questions. Students should use the hints and the Answers and Solutions sections to improve their understanding of how to answer questions about each skill.

- The third and fourth pages of each lesson present GED practice questions that allow students to apply the skill to the same types of questions that they will see on the test.

Students should use the *Answers and Solutions* at the back of this book to check their answers and to learn more about how to make the correct answer choices.

3. Take the *Official GED® Practice Tests Form PA: Mathematics Part I and Part II* in this book and analyze the results.

The half-length practice tests at the end of this book are the Official GED Practice Tests Form PA: Mathematics Part I and Part II–developed by the GED Testing Service®. Taking this test allows students to evaluate how well they will do on the actual GED Mathematics Tests.

Based on the results, test administrators can determine if the student is ready to take the actual test. Those students who are not ready will need more study and should use the other GED Mathematics preparation materials available from Steck-Vaughn, which are listed at the back of this book and can be found at www.SteckVaughn.com/AdultEd.

4. Prior to taking the GED Mathematics Tests, take an additional Official GED Practice Test.

The more experience that students have taking practice tests, the better they will do on the actual test. For additional test practice, they can take the Full-Length Practice Test Form or any of the other Official GED Practice Tests available from Steck-Vaughn at www.SteckVaughn.com/AdultEd.

By using this book and the others in this series, students will have the information and strategies developed by both the GED Testing Service® and experienced adult educators, so that they can reach their goal—passing the GED Tests.

Teaching Tips

Below are suggested interactive teaching strategies that support and develop specific *GED® Key Skills*.

Ratio and Proportion (Mathematics KEY Skill 4)

The teacher and students can bring in maps that contain distance scales.

- Explain how to use a map scale. For example, on a map, 1 inch = 400 miles.

- Demonstrate how to write and solve a proportion to find a distance on a scale drawing or a map. For example, to find out <u>how many miles</u> are represented by 5 inches, the proportion would read:

$$\frac{1 \text{ inch}}{400 \text{ miles}} = \frac{5 \text{ inch}}{x \text{ miles}}$$

Demonstrate how to find <u>how many inches</u> it would take to show 2000 miles. The proportion would be:

$$\frac{1 \text{ inch}}{400 \text{ miles}} = \frac{x \text{ inches}}{2000 \text{ miles}}$$

- Students can write and solve proportions to find distances between places on a map. Students will either need rulers or straight edges to use the scales on the map.

Tables and Charts (Mathematics KEY Skill 6)

The teacher and students can bring in newspapers or other printed ads with the prices of everyday items.

- Discuss what the local sales tax is. Show how to find the total amount of the cost of an item in one step. For example, if the price of a shirt is $39.95 and the tax is 6%, you can multiply $39.95 × 1.06. (Be sure to discuss why this is 1.06.)

- Make a small table that lists the costs of five items and their final prices, including sales tax. Encourage students to use the calculator used on the GED Mathematics Tests to complete the table.

Item	Price	Price with 6% Sales Tax	Price with 7% Sales Tax	Price with 8% Sales Tax
Shirt	$39.95	$42.35		
Automobile	$23,495	$24,904.70		
Computer	$1,200	$1,272		

- Extend the table for an additional 1% and 2%. Observe the impact on the cost of items.

Problem-Solving Challenges

GED Testing Service® research showed that test takers had difficulty with several issues related to problem solving. One issue was "solving multi-step problems" (Mathematics Key Skill 5). Another issue was understanding how to work with the alternative "Not enough information is given." The following problem-solving strategy can be practiced to help with both issues.

Read the problem

1. *What is the question asking me to find?* (Be specific.)

2. *What information do I need to answer the question?*

   NOTE: If there is not enough information, students can select "Not enough information is given."

3. *What do I have to do to solve the problem?*

Solve the problem. Keep labels (such as miles, inches, etc.) with your numbers to see if you have answered the question.

4. *Does my solution answer the question? If I have not answered the question, do I need to take any more steps?*

5. *Does my solution make sense?*

   NOTE: If students keep the labels with their numbers, they may see that they have not answered the question that was asked and may determine that they may still have to complete one or more steps.

Mathematics Pretest

Directions

This pretest consists of 20 questions designed to measure how well you know the skills needed to pass the GED Mathematics Test. There is one question for each of the 20 lessons in this book.

- Take the pretest and record your answers on the *Pretest Answer Sheet* found on page 127. Choose the <u>one best answer</u> to each question.

- Check your answers in the *Pretest Answers and Solutions* section, which starts on page 109. Reading the solution for each problem will help you understand why the correct answers are right and the incorrect answer choices are wrong.

- Formulas you may need are given on page 94. Only some of the questions will require you to use a formula. Not all the formulas given will be needed.

- Fill in the *Pretest Performance Analysis Chart* on page 9 to determine which skills are the most important for you to focus on as you work in this book.

Questions 1 and 2 refer to the following diagram.

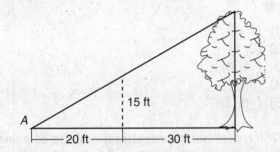

1. A notice in the newspaper states that homeowners with trees taller than 50 feet will pay a fee. In order to determine the height of your tree, you make the diagram above. Which proportion could be used to find the height of your tree?

(1) $\frac{x}{15} = \frac{50}{20}$

(2) $\frac{15}{x} = \frac{50}{20}$

(3) $\frac{15(20)}{50} = \frac{x}{1}$

(4) $\frac{50(20)}{15} = \frac{x}{1}$

(5) Not enough information is given.

 2. What is the distance (in feet) from the top of the tree to point *A* (the hypotenuse of the large triangle)?

(1)   12.5
(2)   26.5
(3)   37.5
(4)   62.5
(5) 3906.25

Question 3 refers to the following figure.

3. The Outfitters Backpacking Association will begin and end their hiking outing at the town of Jackson. Which mixed number below represents the total number of miles that the Outfitters will travel during their hike?

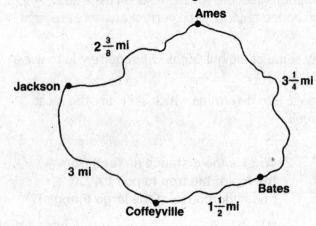

(1) $8\frac{1}{8}$

(2) $9\frac{5}{14}$

(3) $9\frac{8}{9}$

(4) $10\frac{1}{8}$

(5) $10\frac{1}{4}$

Questions 4 and 5 refer to the following coordinate graph.

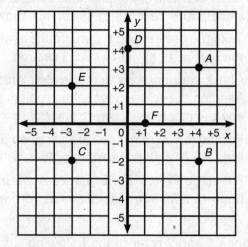

4. Point *F* on the graph refers to which ordered pair?

(1) (1, 0)
(2) (0, 1)
(3) (−1, 0)
(4) (0, −1)
(5) (−3, 2)

5. Which number represents the slope of a line drawn through Point *F* and Point *C*?

(1) −1

(2) $\frac{1}{2}$

(3) 1

(4) 2

(5) 4

6. For one brand of cereal, the nutrition label shows 210 calories for a 1-cup serving of cereal alone and 250 calories for a 1-cup serving with $\frac{1}{2}$ cup skim milk added. By what percent does the number of calories increase when milk is added? Round to the nearest whole percent.

(1) 16%
(2) 19%
(3) 22%
(4) 50%
(5) Not enough information is given.

Question 7 refers to the following line graph.

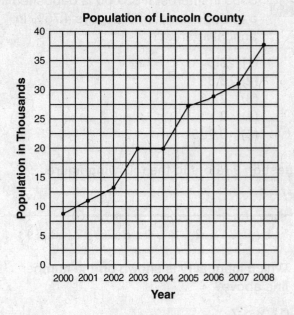

7. Between which two years did the population of Lincoln County increase the most?

(1) 2001 and 2002
(2) 2002 and 2003
(3) 2003 and 2004
(4) 2004 and 2005
(5) 2005 and 2006

8. How many years will it take to earn $335 in interest if $3,000 is deposited in a savings account that pays 4.75% in annual interest?

   (1) 23.5
   (2) 3.35
   (3) 2.35
   (4) 2
   (5) 0.235

Question 9 refers to the following figure.

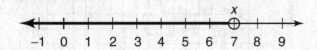

9. Which inequality is shown on the number line above?

   (1) $x > 7$
   (2) $x < 7$
   (3) $x < -7$
   (4) $x \leq 7$
   (5) $x \geq 7$

<u>Question 10</u> refers to this clock.

10. Sarah's favorite class lasts 1 hour 45 minutes and is every Thursday night. If class starts at the time shown, what time will it end?

   (1) 9:15 P.M.
   (2) 8:45 P.M.
   (3) 7:30 A.M.
   (4) 6:30 P.M.
   (5) 5:45 P.M.

11. Eduardo completed $\frac{1}{4}$ of his homework, Keenan completed $\frac{3}{4}$ of his homework, and Sarah completed $\frac{3}{8}$ of her homework. Which list below shows the students in order from the least to greatest amount of homework completed?

(1) Eduardo, Keenan, Sarah
(2) Sarah, Eduardo, Keenan
(3) Keenan, Eduardo, Sarah
(4) Sarah, Keenan, Eduardo
(5) Eduardo, Sarah, Keenan

Question 12 refers to the following figure.

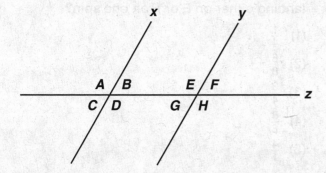

12. If lines *x* and *y* are parallel, which angle is equal to $\angle A$?

(1) $\angle B$
(2) $\angle F$
(3) $\angle C$
(4) $\angle G$
(5) $\angle H$

13. Chen is selling cooking aprons at a kitchen festival for $18.50 each. Which equation could be used to find the total amount of money he will earn, *c*, if he sells *n* aprons?

(1) $c = 18.50n$
(2) $n = 18.50c$
(3) $c = 18.50 + n$
(4) $c = \frac{18.50}{n}$
(5) Not enough information is given.

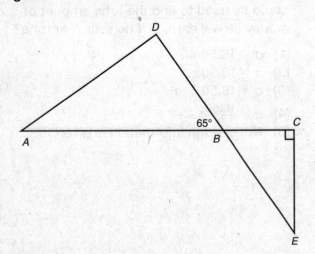

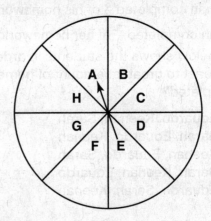

14. What is the angle measure of ∠CEB?

   (1)   25°
   (2)   65°
   (3)   90°
   (4) 100°
   (5) 130°

 15. If $\overline{CE}$ = 14.6 m and $\overline{BC}$ = 9.5 m, what is the perimeter (in meters) of triangle *CBE*? Round your answer to the nearest tenth.

   (1)   17.4
   (2)   24.1
   (3)   41.5
   (4) 213.2
   (5) 303.4

16. What is the probability of the spinner landing either on E or F on one spin?

   (1) $\frac{1}{4}$

   (2) $\frac{6}{8}$

   (3) $\frac{3}{4}$

   (4) $\frac{8}{6}$

   (5) $\frac{4}{1}$

Questions 17 and 18 refer to the following table.

LIFE INSURANCE PREMIUM COSTS	
Age	Annual Cost per $1,000
44	$29.50
45	$30.15
46	$31.50
47	$32.85
48	$33.50

 17. Sally, age 46, wants to buy a $100,000 life insurance policy. Based on the table above, what will be the cost of this coverage for one year?

(1) $ 31.50
(2) $ 32.36
(3) $ 315.00
(4) $ 323.60
(5) $3,150.00

 18. What is the percent increase in annual cost per $1,000 of coverage from age 47 to 48? Round your answer to the nearest tenth of a percent.

(1) 0.02%
(2) 2.0%
(3) 2.7%
(4) 4.3%
(5) 5.0%

19. The length of a field is equal to *x* meters. The width of the field is 20 yards less than the length. Which equation can be used to find the width of the field above if the perimeter is 280 yards?

(1) $2(x - 20) = 280$
(2) $2(x - 20)^2 = 280$
(3) $(x - 20) + 20 = 280$
(4) $2(x - 20) + 2x = 280$
(5) $(x - 20) + 2x = 280$

Question 20 refers to the following bar graph.

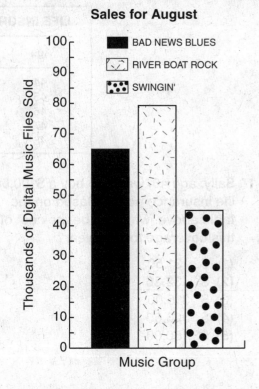

Sales for August

20. Which statement below is true based on information from the graph above?

(1) Bad News Blues outsold Swingin' by 25,000 files.
(2) River Boat Rock outsold Swingin' by only 3,500 files.
(3) Swingin' sold less than 4,500 files in August.
(4) Bad News Blues sold 65,000 files in August.
(5) After an upswing, digital music sales declined in August.

Pretest Performance Analysis Chart

The following chart can help you to determine your strengths and weaknesses on the skill areas needed to pass the GED Mathematics Tests.

- Use the *Pretest Answers and Solutions* on pages 109–110 to check your answers.
- On the chart below:
  - Circle the question numbers that you answered correctly.
  - Put a check mark (✓) next to the skills for which you answered the questions incorrectly.
  - Use the page numbers to find the lessons that you need to target as you work.

Question Number	Skills to Target (✓)	GED Mathematics Skill Lessons	Page Numbers
11		**Skill 1:** Comparing and Ordering Numbers	10–13
3		**Skill 2:** Fractions and Mixed Numbers	14–17
18		**Skill 3:** Percents	18–21
1		**Skill 4:** Ratio and Proportion	22–25
6		**Skill 5:** Multi-Step Problems	26–29
17		**Skill 6:** Tables and Charts	30–33
7		**Skill 7:** Line Graphs	34–37
20		**Skill 8:** Bar and Circle Graphs	38–41
16		**Skill 9:** Probability	42–45
10		**Skill 10:** Elapsed Time	46–49
12		**Skill 11:** Lines and Angles	50–53
14		**Skill 12:** Triangles	54–57
2		**Skill 13:** Pythagorean Theorem	58–61
15		**Skill 14:** Perimeter, Area, and Volume	62–65
4		**Skill 15:** Coordinates	66–69
9		**Skill 16:** Expressions, Equations, and Inequalities	70–73
5		**Skill 17:** Linear Equations	74–77
13		**Skill 18:** Functions	78–81
8		**Skill 19:** Algebraic Formulas	82–85
19		**Skill 20:** Algebra Word Problems	86–89

Skill 1

Comparing and Ordering Numbers

To answer some GED questions, you may need to compare fractions, decimals, or percents. When **comparing** and **ordering** numbers, you can change all of the numbers to decimals to make them easier to work with. To answer some questions, you will need to change numbers from decimals to fractions.

EXAMPLE: Arrange $\frac{2}{5}$, 0.6, and 50% in order from least to greatest.

STEP 1 Change all of the numbers to decimals with the same number of decimal places. Add zeros when necessary so that the numbers all have the same place value.

To convert a fraction to a decimal, divide the numerator by the denominator.

To convert a percent to a decimal, move the decimal point two places to the left.

$$\frac{2}{5} = 2 \div 5 = 0.40 \qquad 0.6 = 0.60 \qquad 50\% = 0.50$$

STEP 2 Put the equivalent values in order from least to greatest.

$$0.40 \qquad 0.50 \qquad 0.60$$

least   *greatest*

STEP 3 Change the decimals back to their original form.

ANSWER: $\frac{2}{5}$, 50%, 0.6

The table to the right shows some commonly used fractions along with their decimal and percent equivalents. Becoming familiar with these commonly used conversions will help you to answer many GED math questions quickly and accurately.

Fraction	Decimal	Percent
$\frac{1}{4}$	0.25	25%
$\frac{1}{2}$	0.5	50%
$\frac{3}{4}$	0.75	75%
$\frac{1}{3}$	0.33	33%
$\frac{2}{3}$	0.67	67%
$\frac{1}{5}$	0.2	20%
$\frac{2}{5}$	0.4	40%
$\frac{3}{5}$	0.6	60%
$\frac{4}{5}$	0.8	80%
$\frac{1}{10}$	0.1	10%
$\frac{5}{10}$	0.5	50%

Practice the Skill

Try these examples. Choose the **one best answer** to each question. Then check your answers and the solutions.

1. Which of the following numbers has the same value as 0.375?

    (1) 3.75%

    (2) $\frac{3}{8}$

    (3) 375%

    (4) $\frac{3}{16}$

    (5) 0.375%

HINT Change all the numbers to the same form to compare.

2. Sergio needed to compare some percents. He compared $6\frac{1}{2}\%$, 6.3%, $6\frac{1}{3}\%$, 6.4%, and $6\frac{1}{4}\%$. Which of these percents is the greatest?

    (1) $6\frac{1}{2}\%$

    (2) 6.3%

    (3) $6\frac{1}{3}\%$

    (4) 6.4%

    (5) $6\frac{1}{4}\%$

Calculator Hint: You can use your calculator to convert a fraction to a percent. To find $6\frac{1}{2}\%$ using your calculator, first find the decimal equivalent of $\frac{1}{2}$. To find $\frac{1}{2}$, key in 1 $\boxed{\div}$ 2 $\boxed{=}$. The screen will display 0.5. Then add 6 to 0.5, which is $6\frac{1}{2}\%$ or 6.50%.

Answers and Solutions

1. (2) $\frac{3}{8}$

Step 1: Convert all the numbers to decimals.

$$3.75\% = 0.0375$$
$$\frac{3}{8} = 0.375$$
$$375\% = 3.75$$
$$\frac{3}{16} = 0.1875$$
$$0.375\% = 0.00375$$

Step 2: Choose the number that is equal to 0.375. The fraction $\frac{3}{8}$ converts to 0.375.

2. (1) $6\frac{1}{2}\%$

Step 1: Change the fraction part of the percents to decimals.

$$6\frac{1}{2} = 6.5\%, \ 6\frac{1}{3} = 6.33\%, \text{ and } 6\frac{1}{4} = 6.25\%$$

Step 2: Add zeros to the end of the decimals to make them all the same place value.

$$6.5\% = 6.50$$
$$6.3\% = 6.30$$
$$6.33\% = 6.33$$
$$6.4\% = 6.40$$
$$6.25\% = 6.25$$

Step 3: Compare. 6.50 is the greatest number, so the answer is $6\frac{1}{2}\%$.

Comparing and Ordering Numbers

Directions: Choose the <u>one best answer</u> to each question.

1. Tom ate $\frac{1}{2}$ of his pizza, Juan ate $\frac{1}{4}$ of his pizza, and DeWayne ate $\frac{5}{8}$ of his pizza. Which list shows the men in order from the least to greatest amount of pizza eaten?

   (1) Tom, Juan, DeWayne
   (2) Juan, Tom, DeWayne
   (3) DeWayne, Tom, Juan
   (4) Juan, DeWayne, Tom
   (5) Tom, DeWayne, Juan

Questions 2 and 3 refer to this figure.

 2. Which of the price tags will give you the best buy?

   (1) 3 for $1.00
   (2) $0.30 each
   (3) 4 for $1.25
   (4) $0.35 each
   (5) $0.25 each

 3. Which fraction below is greater than the greatest unit cost of the price tags?

   (1) $\frac{2}{5}$

   (2) $\frac{2}{6}$

   (3) $\frac{3}{10}$

   (4) $\frac{2}{7}$

   (5) $\frac{3}{9}$

Question 4 refers to this figure.

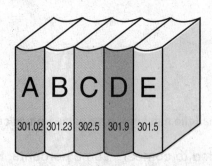

4. Library books are organized from least to greatest according to their decimal numbers. Which books need to change places to ensure that the books are in order?

   (1) A and B
   (2) B and D
   (3) C and E
   (4) D and A
   (5) E and B

 5. The ratio of students to teachers in five schools was listed in the newspaper.

Mina	62:3
Cedar	74:4
Fox	47:2
Rosewood	26:1
Travis	51:2

   Which school has the fewest students per teacher?

   (1) Mina
   (2) Cedar
   (3) Fox
   (4) Rosewood
   (5) Not enough information is given.

Questions 6 and 7 refer to this map.

The map below shows the distances in miles between several towns.

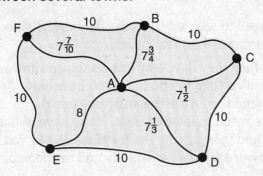

6. On the map above, which town is closest to Town A?

   (1) Town B
   (2) Town C
   (3) Town D
   (4) Town E
   (5) Town F

7. Raquel drives to nearby towns for her job. She lives in Town A. Which trip would be less than 25 miles round trip?

   (1) A → B → C → A
   (2) A → C → D → A
   (3) A → D → E → A
   (4) A → E → F → A
   (5) Not enough information is given.

 8. Melita read $\frac{5}{8}$ of her book, Roberta read 60% of her book, and Sofie read $\frac{2}{3}$ of her book. Which list below shows the women in order from the greatest to least amount of their book read?

   (1) Melita, Roberta, Sofie
   (2) Roberta, Sofie, Melita
   (3) Sofie, Roberta, Melita
   (4) Sofie, Melita, Roberta
   (5) Roberta, Melita, Sofie

9. Tyrone wants to buy the two packages of chicken that weigh the most. The following packages are available:

   Package A   1.34 lb

   Package B $1\frac{1}{2}$ lb

   Package C $1\frac{1}{4}$ lb

   Package D   1.7 lb

   Which two packages weigh the most?

   (1) A and B
   (2) A and C
   (3) B and C
   (4) B and D
   (5) C and D

 10. Tanisha is shipping some packages. She can only afford to ship the lightest package today. The three packages weigh $4\frac{5}{8}$ pounds, $4\frac{7}{16}$ pounds, and 4.375 pounds. Which weight is the lightest?

Mark your answer in the circles in the grid below.

⊘	⊘	⊘	
·	·	·	·	·
⓪	⓪	⓪	⓪	⓪
①	①	①	①	①
②	②	②	②	②
③	③	③	③	③
④	④	④	④	④
⑤	⑤	⑤	⑤	⑤
⑥	⑥	⑥	⑥	⑥
⑦	⑦	⑦	⑦	⑦
⑧	⑧	⑧	⑧	⑧
⑨	⑨	⑨	⑨	⑨

> **TIP**
>
> When reading word problems, look for cue words that will tell you if you're looking for the greatest or least value. Words such as *most, highest,* and *farthest* tell you to look for the greatest amount. Words such as *less, best deal,* and *closest* tell you to look for the smallest amount.

Answers and solutions start on page 111.

Numbers, Number Sense, and Operations

Fractions and Mixed Numbers

To answer some GED questions, you may need to add, subtract, multiply, and divide **fractions** and **mixed numbers.** Here are some helpful reminders.

Fractions can be added or subtracted only when they have a **common denominator.** Fractions with common denominators are called "like fractions." If you have like fractions, add or subtract the **numerators,** and then write the answer above the common denominator. If needed, reduce the result to lowest terms. If you have unlike fractions, find a common denominator first and then rewrite the fractions. When you add or subtract with mixed numbers, work with each part separately and then combine the results.

When multiplying or dividing fractions, you do not need to have a common denominator. To multiply fractions, multiply the numerators across the top and the denominators across the bottom.

Division is the inverse (opposite) of multiplication. You can use multiplication to solve a division problem. First **invert** the divisor, or turn it upside down. Then solve just as you would a multiplication problem—multiply the numerators and denominators across. To divide with mixed numbers, first convert the mixed number to an **improper fraction.**

EXAMPLE: A road sign shows that Ettaville is exactly $1\frac{3}{4}$ miles due east and Wollatown is exactly $2\frac{1}{2}$ miles due west. What is the distance between the two towns?

STEP 1 Add the whole numbers.

$$1 + 2 = 3$$

STEP 2 Find a common denominator for the fractions.

$$\frac{1}{2} \times \frac{2}{2} = \frac{2}{4}$$

STEP 3 Then add the fractions with the common denominators.

$$\frac{2}{4} + \frac{3}{4} = \frac{5}{4} = 1\frac{1}{4}$$

STEP 4 Add the whole number results from Step 1 and Step 3.

$$3 + 1 = 4$$

STEP 5 Add the fraction from the result in Step 3 ($\frac{1}{4}$) to the whole number in Step 4 (4).

$$\frac{1}{4} + 4 = 4\frac{1}{4}$$

ANSWER: $4\frac{1}{4}$ miles

Practice the Skill

1. On Monday, Wednesday, and Friday, Ravi exercises for $1\frac{2}{3}$ hours. On Tuesday and Thursday, he exercises for $\frac{1}{2}$ hour. How many total hours does he exercise in a week?

   (1) $\frac{5}{3}$

   (2) $4\frac{1}{2}$

   (3) 5

   (4) $5\frac{1}{2}$

   (5) 6

HINT To convert a mixed number to an improper fraction, multiply the denominator by the whole number. Then add the numerator to the product. This sum is the numerator of the improper fraction.

2. Gina has $2\frac{1}{2}$ acres on which she plans to grow 3 different crops. If she wants to divide the land equally among the three crops, how many acres should she allow per crop?

   (1) $5\frac{1}{2}$

   (2) 3

   (3) $\frac{5}{2}$

   (4) $\frac{5}{6}$

   (5) Not enough information is given.

 Calculator Hint: Use the $\boxed{a^{b/c}}$ key to enter a mixed number into your calculator. To input $2\frac{1}{2}$ into your calculator, key in 2 $\boxed{a^{b/c}}$ 1 $\boxed{a^{b/c}}$ 2.

Answers and Solutions

1. (5) 6

Step 1: Convert $1\frac{2}{3}$ to an improper fraction.
$$1\frac{2}{3} = \frac{5}{3}$$

Step 2: Calculate hours for M, W, F.
$$3 \times \frac{5}{3} = \frac{15}{3} = 5$$

Step 3: Calculate hours for T, TH.
$$2 \times \frac{1}{2} = 1$$

Step 4: Add the results from Step 2 and Step 3.
$$5 + 1 = 6$$

2. (4) $\frac{5}{6}$

Step 1: Convert $2\frac{1}{2}$ to an improper fraction.
$$2\frac{1}{2} = \frac{5}{2}$$

Step 2: Divide the result from Step 1 ($\frac{5}{2}$) by 3. Remember to invert the 3.
$$\frac{5}{2} \div 3 = \frac{5}{2} \times \frac{1}{3}$$

Step 3: Cross multiply the numerators and denominators.
$$\frac{5}{2} \times \frac{1}{3} = \frac{5 \times 1}{2 \times 3} = \frac{5}{6}$$

Fractions and Mixed Numbers

Directions: Choose the one best answer to each question.

Questions 1 and 2 refer to this table.

Joanne's Monthly Budget	
Rent	$\frac{3}{10}$ of Income
Car Payment	$\frac{1}{4}$ of Income
Food	$\frac{1}{5}$ of Income
Clothes	$\frac{1}{10}$ of Income
Other Bils	$\frac{3}{20}$ of Income

1. How much of Joanne's income is spent on rent, car payment, and other bills combined?

   (1) $\frac{1}{5}$

   (2) $\frac{1}{4}$

   (3) $\frac{3}{10}$

   (4) $\frac{11}{20}$

   (5) $\frac{7}{10}$

 2. How much more of Joanne's income is spent on food than on clothes?

   (1) $\frac{3}{10}$

   (2) $\frac{1}{5}$

   (3) $\frac{1}{10}$

   (4) $\frac{1}{15}$

   (5) $\frac{1}{20}$

3. Joshua has a 15-day ski pass. He has skied for $6\frac{1}{2}$ days. Which expression shows how many more days he can ski?

   (1) $15 - 6 + \frac{1}{2}$

   (2) $14\frac{2}{2} - 6\frac{1}{2}$

   (3) $14\frac{2}{2} - 6 + \frac{1}{2}$

   (4) $15\frac{2}{2} - 6 - \frac{1}{2}$

   (5) Not enough information is given.

 4. Colette has 8 hours vacation time. She used $5\frac{1}{4}$ hours to attend an art show. How many hours does she have left?

   (1) $2\frac{3}{4}$

   (2) 3

   (3) $3\frac{1}{4}$

   (4) $3\frac{3}{4}$

   (5) $13\frac{1}{4}$

5. Jane is on a trail that ends at the river. If Jane's horse averages $7\frac{1}{2}$ miles per hour, how many hours will it take her to ride to the river?

   (1) 2

   (2) 3

   (3) 4

   (4) 5

   (5) Not enough information is given.

6. Hector purchased enough fertilizer to cover $\frac{1}{2}$ his cropland. He has $8\frac{1}{4}$ acres of cropland. How can he determine the number of acres he can fertilize?

   (1) Divide $\frac{1}{2}$ by $8\frac{1}{4}$ acres.

   (2) Multiply 2 by $8\frac{1}{4}$ acres.

   (3) Divide $\frac{33}{4}$ by $\frac{1}{4}$.

   (4) Multiply $\frac{33}{4}$ by $\frac{1}{2}$.

   (5) Not enough information is given.

Questions 7 and 8 refer to this table.

Project Alpha	
Employee	**Weekly Hours**
Samantha	$4\frac{1}{4}$
Peter	$5\frac{4}{8}$
Sylvia	$8\frac{3}{4}$
David	$10\frac{1}{2}$

 7. If the employees doubled their hours, what would be their total number of hours worked on the project per week?

    (1) 20
    (2) 29
    (3) 38
    (4) 44
    (5) 58

8. If Samantha and David each earn $12 per hour, how much do they earn altogether each week?

    (1) $ 51
    (2) $ 126
    (3) $ 177
    (4) $ 321
    (5) $ 2124

Questions 9 and 10 refer to this table.

Joe's lumberyard sells lumber in the sizes shown in the table below.

Size	Length in feet	Width in inches
2 × 4	8, 10, 12, 16	$3\frac{1}{2}$
2 × 6	8, 10, 12, 16	$5\frac{1}{2}$
1 × 2	6, 8, 10	$1\frac{1}{2}$
1 × 4	6, 8, 10	$3\frac{1}{2}$

 9. Dayla decides to make a 10-foot long plant shelf for her porch. If she uses 5 pieces of 1 × 4 lumber in 10-foot lengths, what will be the width of the shelf in inches?

    (1) 12
    (2) $15\frac{1}{2}$
    (3) $17\frac{1}{2}$
    (4) $20\frac{1}{2}$
    (5) Not enough information is given.

 10. How many 2 × 6 pieces of 16-foot lumber will Dayla need to surface a covered porch if the porch measures 16 feet by 14 feet? Round to the nearest whole piece.

Mark your answer in the circles in the grid below.

Answers and solutions start on page 111.

KEY Skill 3

Percents

Many GED problems are percent problems. An easy way to remember the formula to calculate **percents** is to use the percent triangle. The percent triangle shows the relationship between the **part, rate,** and **base.** The symbols in the triangle indicate when to multiply ($\times$) and when to divide ($\div$). You can find the part, rate, and base by following the steps below. When finding the part or base, remember to first change the percent, or rate, to a decimal.

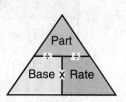

Find the part of a whole amount: Multiply the base by the rate.

$$Part = Base \times Rate$$

Find the base(the whole amount): Divide the part by the rate.

$$Base = \frac{Part}{Rate}$$

Find the rate (the percent): Divide the part by the base.

$$Rate = \frac{Part}{Base}$$

The result for rate will be a decimal. To express the rate as a percent, multiply by 100, or move the decimal point two places to the right. Add the % sign.

EXAMPLE 1: What is 20% of $15.00?

STEP 1 Change 20% to a rate by dividing by 100 and dropping the % sign.

$$20\% \div 100 = 0.20$$

STEP 2 Find the part by using the formula *Part = Base $\times$ Rate.*

$$Part = 0.20 \times \$15.00 = \$3.00$$

ANSWER: $3.00

EXAMPLE 2: $4.50 is what percent of $30.00?

STEP 1 Find the rate by using the formula:

$$Rate = \frac{Part}{Base}$$

$$Rate = \frac{\$4.50}{\$30.00} = 0.15$$

STEP 2 Convert the rate to a percent by multiplying by 100, and then add a % sign.

$$0.15 \times 100 = 15\%$$

ANSWER: 15%

Practice the Skill

1. Joan made a $750 down payment on a used car that sells for $7500. Which expression can be used to find the down payment as a percent of the price of the car?

   (1) $750 × $7500 × 100
   (2) $750 ÷ $7500 × 100
   (3) $7500 ÷ $750 × 100
   (4) $7500 − $750 × 100
   (5) $7500 + $750 × 100

HINT Decide whether you need to find the part, the base (the whole), or the rate (percent). Then choose the method from the percent triangle, and substitute for the known numbers.

2. If your food bill at a restaurant is $18.27 and you want to leave a 15% tip, the tip will be between what two amounts?

   (1) $0.50 and $1.00
   (2) $1.00 and $1.50
   (3) $1.50 and $2.00
   (4) $2.00 and $2.50
   (5) $2.50 and $3.00

Calculator Hint: To find the percent on a calculator, subtract the percent from the total. Key in
18.27 × 15 [SHIFT] [%] [=]. The screen will display 15% of $18.27.

Answers and Solutions

1. (2) $750 ÷ $7500 × 100
Step 1: Find the percent (rate). Divide the down payment (part), $750, by the price (base), $7500.

$$Rate = Part ÷ Base$$
$$Rate = \$750 ÷ \$7500$$

Step 2: To convert to a percent, multiply your answer from Step 1 by 100.

$$\$750 ÷ \$7500 × 100$$

2. (5) $2.50 and $3.00
Step 1: Convert the percent to a decimal by dividing by 100. Drop the percent sign.

$$15\% ÷ 100 = 0.15$$

Step 2: Find the actual tip.

$$\$18.27 = 0.15 = \$2.74$$

Step 3: Choose the range where $2.74 belongs, which is **between $2.50 and $3.00.**

Percents

Directions: Choose the one best answer to each question.

1. A store is having a 10% off sale. By what amount will the price of the shirt be reduced?

$35

$66

$27

(1) $0.35
(2) $0.66
(3) $2.70
(4) $3.50
(5) $6.60

2. An insurance company paid $1200 of a $1500 repair bill for Pat's car. What percent of the bill did the company pay?

(1) 1.25%
(2) 8%
(3) 12.5%
(4) 20%
(5) 80%

3. In an election, one of the candidates received 19% of the votes. Which expression could be used to estimate the number of votes the candidate received if 25,978 people voted in the election?

(1) 26,000 ÷ 20
(2) 26,000(20)
(3) 26,000(0.20)
(4) 26(2)
(5) 26 ÷ 0.2

4. Jenny wants to buy a digital music player for $49.95. If sales tax is 8.25%, about how much tax will she pay on the digital music player?

(1) $ 0.17
(2) $ 0.41
(3) $ 4.12
(4) $ 54.07
(5) $412.09

5. A store buys a computer from the manufacturer. The store then sells the computer for its cost plus a 25% markup. What is the cost of the computer from the manufacturer?

For Sale
$1500

(1) $1200
(2) $1475
(3) $1500
(4) $1525
(5) Not enough information is given.

> **TIP**
>
> To help you answer percent problems on the GED Mathematics Tests, draw the percent triangle on the scratch paper that will be provided when you take the test.

6. Brian bought a used car for $3500. A month later he sold the car for $3000, a loss of $500. His selling price was approximately what percent of the original cost of the car? Round your answer to the nearest whole percent.

(1) 86%
(2) 35%
(3) 30%
(4) 17%
(5) 14%

Questions 7 and 8 refer to this bill.

Robin's Restaurant

2 - Lunch Special	= $5.99
1 - Orange Juice	= $1.99
Subtotal	= $13.97
Tip =	$3.00
Total =	$16.97

7. The subtotal of the bill for Sue and Joyce's lunch was $13.97. Which expression can be used to estimate the tip as a percent of the subtotal?

(1) 14 ÷ 3 × 100
(2) 14 + 3
(3) 3 ÷ 14 × 100
(4) 14 − 3 ÷ 100
(5) Not enough information is given.

8. Sue has already ordered 1 orange juice, which is already on the bill. If Joyce later decides to order an orange juice, and they leave an 18% tip, what will be the new total?

(1) $ 2.87
(2) $ 3.00
(3) $15.96
(4) $18.83
(5) $18.96

9. Last year 1245 people attended the annual Springtown fair. This year 249 more people attended. Which expression can be used to find the percent increase in the Springtown fair attendance this year?

(1) 249 ÷ 1245
(2) 249 ÷ 1245 × 100
(3) 1245 ÷ 249 × 100
(4) (249 + 1245) ÷ 1245 × 100
(5) 1245 ÷ (249 + 1245) × 100

10. The nutrition label on a granola bar reads 250 calories, with 135 of those calories from carbohydrates. What percent of the calories are from carbohydrates?

(1) 1.8%
(2) 11.5%
(3) 18%
(4) 54%
(5) 57%

11. Raul purchased stock with a value of $32.50 per share. Six months later, the stock's value has risen to 112% of that value. What is the new value of each share of the stock?

Mark your answer in the circles in the grid below.

Answers and solutions start on page 112.

KEY Skill 4

Ratio and Proportion

A **ratio** shows a relationship between two numbers, such as 3 teachers for 21 students. Ratios can be written in three ways: 3 to 21, 3:21, or $\frac{3}{21}$. Ratios can be reduced without changing the relationship between the two numbers. This means $\frac{3}{21}$ is the same as $\frac{1}{7}$.

A **proportion** is two ratios of equal value, such as $\frac{6}{8} = \frac{3}{4}$. You can check if two ratios are equal by using **cross multiplication.** The numerator of the first ratio multiplied by the denominator of the second ratio must be equal to the numerator of the second ratio multiplied by the denominator of the first ratio.

$$\frac{6}{8} = \frac{3}{4}$$
$$6 \times 4 = 3 \times 8$$
$$24 = 24$$

If the relationship between two numbers is given, and an equal relationship needs to be found, you can set up a proportion to solve the problem. For example, if you know that 12 inches is equal to 1 foot, you can find the number of inches in 5 feet.

$$\frac{12 \text{ in.}}{1 \text{ ft}} = \frac{n \text{ in.}}{5 \text{ ft}}$$
$$n \times 1 = 12 \times 5$$
$$n = 60 \text{ inches}$$

EXAMPLE 1: If 6 apples cost $1.50, what expression shows how much 9 apples cost?

STEP 1   Write the ratio of apples to cost.

$$\frac{6 \text{ apples}}{\$1.50}$$

STEP 2   Set up a second ratio that has 9 apples and an unknown cost, n.

$$\frac{9 \text{ apples}}{n}$$

STEP 3   Write a proportion with numbers and labels for the two equal ratios.

ANSWER: $\frac{6 \text{ apples}}{\$1.50} = \frac{9 \text{ apples}}{n}$

EXAMPLE 2: If DVDs are 3 for $10.00, what is the approximate cost of 1 DVD?

STEP 1   Set up ratios for 3 DVDs and their cost and for 1 DVD and an unknown cost, c. Then set up a proportion with the two equal ratios.

$$\frac{3 \text{ DVDs}}{\$10.00} = \frac{1 \text{ DVD}}{c}$$

STEP 2   Cross multiply, and then divide to solve for c.

$$c \times 3 \text{ DVDs} = \$10.00 \times 1 \text{ DVD}$$
$$c = \frac{1 \text{ DVD}}{3 \text{ DVDs}} \times \$10.00$$
$$c = \$10.00 \div 3 = \$3.33$$

ANSWER: $3.33

Practice the Skill

Try these examples. Choose the **one best answer** to each question. Then check your answers and the solutions.

1. If a gasoline and oil mixture for a lawn mower is 40 parts gasoline to 1 part oil, which expression shows how many parts oil must be used for 10 parts gasoline?

(1) 10×40
(2) 40×10
(3) $40 \div 1$
(4) $10 \div 40$
(5) $10 \div 4$

HINT Set up a proportion between two ratios of gasoline to oil.

2. If 10 pounds of potatoes sell for $1.70, how much will 5 pounds cost?

(1) $ 0.34
(2) $ 0.85
(3) $ 1.70
(4) $ 3.40
(5) $17.00

 Calculator Hint: To convert a ratio, such as 5:10, to a decimal using your calculator, key in: 5 ÷ 10 = . The screen will display 0.5.

Answers and Solutions

1. (4) $10 \div 40$

Step 1: Set up a ratio of gasoline to oil.

$$\frac{40 \text{ parts gasoline}}{1 \text{ part oil}}$$

Step 2: Set up a ratio for the unknown amount of oil.

$$\frac{10 \text{ parts gasoline}}{? \text{ parts oil}}$$

Step 3: Write a proportion with the two equal ratios.

$$\frac{40 \text{ parts gasoline}}{1 \text{ part oil}} = \frac{10 \text{ parts gasoline}}{? \text{ parts oil}}$$

Step 4: Cross multiply and divide to set up the equation to find the parts of oil needed for 10 parts gasoline.

$$40 \times ? = 10 \times 1$$

$$? = 10 \div 40$$

2. (2) $0.85

Step 1: Set up a ratio of potatoes to cost.

$$\frac{10 \text{ potatoes}}{\$1.70}$$

Step 2: Set up a ratio of 5 potatoes to an unknown cost, c.

$$\frac{5 \text{ potatoes}}{c}$$

Step 3: Write a proportion with the two equal ratios.

$$\frac{10 \text{ potatoes}}{\$1.70} = \frac{5 \text{ potatoes}}{c}$$

Step 4: Find the cross product and divide by the remaining term.

$$5 \text{ potatoes} \times \$1.70 = \$8.50$$
$$\$8.50 \div 10 \text{ potatoes} = \$0.85$$
$$c = \$0.85$$

Ratio and Proportion

Directions: Choose the <u>one best answer</u> to each question.

1. On a map, the scale reads $\frac{1}{4}$ inch = 10 miles. How many miles apart are two cities if the distance between them on the map is 2.5 inches?

   (1) 10
   (2) 25
   (3) 40
   (4) 100
   (5) 250

2. A package of 6 light bulbs sells for $2.79. What is the cost of 2 light bulbs rounded to the nearest cent?

   (1) $0.18
   (2) $0.45
   (3) $0.93
   (4) $3.72
   (5) Not enough information given.

<u>Questions 3 and 4 refer to this figure.</u>

3. What is the ratio of the shaded squares to the unshaded squares of the figure?

   (1) $\frac{12}{25}$
   (2) $\frac{13}{25}$
   (3) $\frac{13}{12}$
   (4) $\frac{12}{13}$
   (5) $\frac{25}{13}$

4. If one more row of squares were added to the bottom of the figure, what would be the new ratio of shaded squares to unshaded squares?

   (1) 15:14
   (2) 16:15
   (3) 15:16
   (4) 1:1
   (5) 14:15

5. A 3-inch-by-4-inch photograph has been enlarged proportionately from size A to size B, as shown in the illustration below. What is the measure of x in inches?

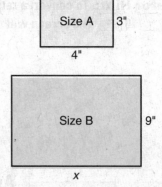

   (1) 12
   (2) 8
   (3) 6
   (4) 4
   (5) Not enough information is given.

TIP

When you set up a proportion, label each number in the ratio with the words that identify the units (*dollars, potatoes,* etc.). This will help you set up the proportion correctly.

6. Martha needs 2.5 yards of fabric to make 2 pillows. Which proportion can be used to find the number of yards of fabric she needs to make 3 pillows?

(1) $\frac{2.5}{2} = \frac{n}{3}$

(2) $\frac{2.5}{3} = \frac{2}{n}$

(3) $\frac{2.5}{2} = \frac{3}{n}$

(4) $\frac{3}{2} = \frac{2.5}{n}$

(5) $\frac{2}{3} = \frac{n}{2.5}$

 7. Last week Ricardo worked 25 hours and earned $205. At the same rate, how much will Ricardo earn this week if he works 35 hours?

Mark your answer in the circles in the grid below.

8. If Crail's chickens lay 8 eggs in 2 days, how many days will it take for Crail to get a dozen eggs?

(1) 7

(2) 6

(3) 5

(4) 4

(5) 3

9. A movie theater usually sells two children's tickets for every three adult tickets. A new blockbuster movie is coming out, and the theater expects to sell 900 adult tickets this week. Which proportion could be used to find the number of children's tickets expected to sell this week?

(1) $\frac{3}{2} = \frac{900}{t}$

(2) $\frac{3}{2} = \frac{t}{900}$

(3) $\frac{2}{3} = \frac{900}{t}$

(4) $\frac{2}{900} = \frac{t}{3}$

(5) $\frac{2}{900} = \frac{t}{3}$

10. The scale on the plan for the birdhouse below is 2 squares equal 5 inches. What is the actual length of the birdhouse in inches?

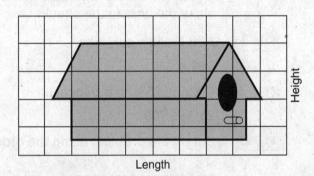

(1) 10

(2) 12

(3) 12.5

(4) 16.25

(5) 25

Answers and solutions start on page 113.

KEY Skill 5

Multi-Step Problems

Many questions on the GED Mathematics Tests require more than one operation to set up or solve the problem. Perform operations in the proper sequence to get the correct answer to these **multi-step problems.** Remember the following rules.

Order of Operations

1. Do all the operations within parentheses.
   $(3 + 2)^2 \times 6 - 5 + 2$ becomes $5^2 \times 6 - 5 + 2$

2. Evaluate terms containing exponents or roots.
   $5^2 \times 6 - 5 + 2$ becomes $25 \times 6 - 5 + 2$

3. Do all multiplication or division in order from left to right.
   $25 \times 6 - 5 + 2$ becomes $150 - 5 + 2$

4. Do all addition or subtraction in order from left to right.
   $150 - 5 + 2 = 147$

EXAMPLE 1: Frank earned $69 last week and $121 this week. What expression would show the amount he should save if he wants to save 25% of his earnings?

STEP 1 Add Frank's earnings.

$69 + $121

STEP 2 Change 25% to a decimal.

$25\% \div 100 = 0.25$

STEP 3 Set up the problem using the order of operations.

ANSWER: ($69 + $121) $\times$ 0.25

EXAMPLE 2: Morgan buys 3 pairs of socks for $1.29 each and a pair of shoes for $29.95. The sales tax is 8%. What is the total amount she spends, including tax?

STEP 1 Set up an expression to find the total cost of the items without tax.

$3 \times $1.29 + 29.95

STEP 2 Then include the sales tax by multiplying the cost of all the items by 0.08.

$(3 \times $1.29 + $29.95) \times 0.08$

STEP 3 Follow the order of operations to solve for the total cost of the items and sales tax.

$(\$3.87 + \$29.95) \times 0.08 \longrightarrow \$33.82 \times 0.08 = \$2.71$

$33.82 is the total cost before tax, and $2.71 is the sales tax.

STEP 4 Add the sales tax to the total cost of the items before tax.

$\$33.82 + \$2.71 = \$36.53$

ANSWER: $36.53

Practice the Skill

1. Dawn is paid $7 per hour for regular hours and $10.50 per hour for overtime. Which expression shows how much Dawn will earn if she works 35 regular hours and 6 hours of overtime?

   (1) $(7 + 10.5) \times (35 + 6)$
   (2) $7 + 10.5 \times 35 + 6$
   (3) $7(35) + 6(10.5)$
   (4) $7(35 + 6)$
   (5) $7 + 10.5 \times (35 + 6)$

   HINT Separate the two pay rates with their corresponding type of hours.

2. The Langleys spend 40% of their monthly income on rent and utilities and another 25% on food. If their monthly income is $2000, how much is left each month for other expenses?

   (1) $ 500
   (2) $ 700
   (3) $ 800
   (4) $1200
   (5) $1300

   Calculator Hint: To find a percent of a whole number, use $\boxed{}^{\text{SHIFT}}$ $\boxed{=}^{\%}$. To find 30% of 2500, key in 2500 $\boxed{\times}$ 30 $\boxed{}^{\text{SHIFT}}$ $\boxed{=}^{\%}$. The display will read 750, which is 30% of 2500.

Answers and Solutions

1. (3) 7(35) + 6(10.5)
Step 1: Multiply the pay rate for regular hours by the number of regular hours Dawn works.

$$\$7 \times 35$$

Step 2: Multiply the pay rate for overtime hours by the number of overtime hours Dawn works.

$$\$10.5 \times 6$$

Step 3: Add the two expressions together.

$$7(35) + 6(10.5)$$

2. (5) $700
Step 1: Convert the percents to decimals and then add.

$$40\% + 25\% \rightarrow 0.40 + 0.25 = 0.65$$

Step 2: Multiply the total percent by the Langleys' monthly income.

$$0.65 \times \$2000 = \$1300$$

Step 3: Subtract the amount of money spent on rent and utilities and food from the total monthly income.

$$\$2000 - \$1300 = \mathbf{\$700}$$

Multi-Step Problems

Directions: Choose the <u>one best answer</u> to each question.

1. Ms. Johnson started the week with $426.79 in her checking account. During the week she wrote one check for $63.97, another check for $27.04, and withdrew $50 in cash. How much did she have left in her account?

   (1) $141 .01
   (2) $285.78
   (3) $312.82
   (4) $335.78
   (5) $385.78

2. The price of movie tickets is $8.50 for evening shows and half price for afternoon shows. On Saturday, 346 tickets were sold for the evening show and 123 tickets were sold for the afternoon show. Which expression represents the total amount collected on Saturday?

   (1) 346(0.5) + 123(8.50)
   (2) 346(8.50 + 123)
   (3) 346 + 123
   (4) 346(8.50) + 123(8.50)
   (5) 346(8.50) + 123 (8.50 ÷ 2)

3. A trail mix contains 2.5 cups of peanuts, 2 cups of raisins, 2 cups of pretzel sticks, and 1.5 cups of banana chips. What percent of the mix is raisins?

   (1) 25%
   (2) 37.5%
   (3) 50%
   (4) 75%
   (5) 87.5%

Questions 4 and 5 refer to these figures.

4"

5"

4. The area of the smaller square is what percent of the area of the larger square?

   (1) 16%
   (2) 25%
   (3) 64%
   (4) 75%
   (5) 80%

5. What percent of the area of the larger square is the area of a triangle with a base equal to 5 inches and a height equal to 5 inches?

   (1) 12.5%
   (2) 25%
   (3) 37.5%
   (4) 50%
   (5) 55%

> **TIP**
>
> When solving multi-step problems, write all the steps of the equation in one expression. Then you can use the order of operations to calculate the answer correctly.

Questions 6 and 7 refer to this figure.

Ingredients	Parts
Sunflower seeds	4
Flax seeds	3
Alfalfa seeds	2
Millet	1

6. Sunflower seeds, flax seeds, alfalfa seeds, and millet are mixed to make Gus's Bird Food for Small Birds using the ratios in the table above. How many pounds of sunflower seeds would be used to make 20 pounds of mix?

(1)   2 pounds
(2)   4 pounds
(3)   6 pounds
(4)   8 pounds
(5) 10 pounds

7. The formula for Gus's Bird Food for Large Birds is different. There are no alfalfa seeds —instead extra millet is used. If 30 pounds of the mix is made, what expression would be used to find the amount of millet that is needed?

(1) (0.10 + 0.20)30
(2) 0.10 + 0.30 × 30
(3) 0.10 + (0.20 × 0.30)
(4) (0.10 + 0.30)30
(5) Not enough information is given.

8. Enrique's salary last year was $400 per week. This year his salary is $480 per week. Which of the following expressions can be used to find the percent of the increase?

(1) 100 − (480 − 400) ÷ 400
(2) 400 ÷ 480 × 100
(3) 480 ÷ 400 × 100
(4) (480 − 400) ÷ 480
(5) (480 − 400) ÷ 400 × 100

9. In a recent election, 78% of the population of Wyldwood voted. Which expression represents the number of people who did not vote if there are 5000 people in Wyldwood?

(1) 5000 − 0.78(5000)
(2) 5000 − 0.22(5000)
(3) 1 − 0.78(5000)
(4) 0.78(5000)
(5) 0.22(0.78)(5000)

10. A $30 item in a store is on sale for 30% off. At the register, an additional 10% is deducted from the sale price. What is the cost of the item after the two markdowns?

Mark your answer in the circles in the grid below.

11. A radio is on sale for 25% off. If there is a 7% sales tax, how much will you pay for the radio?

(1) $30.00
(2) $32.10
(3) $37.00
(4) $27.90
(5) Not enough information is given.

Answers and solutions start on page 114.

Tables and Charts

On the GED test, the information needed to solve some problems is given in a table or chart. **Tables** and **charts** are helpful because they organize **data** in a specific way or they provide an easy way to show a large amount of data. Tables and charts have a title that describes the data. Tables and charts also have **labels** and/or **headings** that show you the difference between different data. Look at the table below.

Mortgage Payment Table Monthly Payments at 8% Annual Interest for 15- and 30-Year Repayment Periods		
Amount Borrowed	15-year Mortgage	30-year Mortgage
$25,000	$238.91	$183.44
30,000	286.70	220.13
35,000	334.48	256.82
40,000	382.26	293.51
45,000	430.04	330.19
50,000	477.83	366.88

Here's how to read this table: To find the amount of monthly payments on $40,000 for a 30-year mortgage, find $40,000 in the *Amount Borrowed* column. Then read across the table to the *30-year Mortgage* column. The amount of the monthly payments is $293.51.

Use the sample table above to answer the two example questions below.

EXAMPLE 1: Troy and Maria's budget allows for no more than a $350 monthly mortgage payment. What is the greatest amount they can borrow if they choose a 30-year mortgage?

STEP 1 Find the column for 30-year mortgages. Look down the column. Find the greatest monthly payment that is less than $350.

STEP 2 Look left across the same row that has the monthly payment you've chosen. Find the amount in the *Amount Borrowed* column that is in the same row.

ANSWER: $45,000

EXAMPLE 2: How much less are the monthly payments for a 30-year mortgage than for the 15-year mortgage if the amount borrowed is $35,000?

STEP 1 Find $35,000 in the *Amount Borrowed* column. Then look across that row to find the corresponding payments in the *15-year* and *30-year Mortgage* columns.

STEP 2 Subtract the 30-year mortgage amount from the 15-year mortgage amount.

$$\$334.48 - \$256.82$$

ANSWER: $77.66

Practice the Skill

Try these examples. Choose the <u>one best answer</u> to each question. Then check your answers and the solutions.

<u>Questions 1 and 2</u> refer to this table.

1. According to the table, how many quarts of potting mixture will you make if you use 4 quarts of garden soil?

   (1)   8
   (2) 10
   (3) 11
   (4) 12
   (5) 14

Potting Soil Mixture	
Quarts	Ingredients
4	garden soil
3	peat moss
2	compost
2	vermiculite

HINT Look at the ratio between all the ingredients.

2. If Kim Lee uses 8 quarts of garden soil, how many quarts of peat moss will she use?

   (1) 3
   (2) 4
   (3) 5
   (4) 6
   (5) Not enough information is given.

Calculator Hint: Set up a proportion to solve this problem: $\frac{4}{3} = \frac{8}{x}$. To find the value of x, press
3 × 8 ÷ 4 = . The screen will display the value of x.

Answers and Solutions

1. (3) 11
Step 1: Find garden soil in the *Ingredients* column. Four quarts of garden soil are used to make one batch of potting soil mixture.

Step 2: Find the ratio of the quarts of garden soil you use to quarts of garden soil in the potting soil mixture.

   you use:in potting mixture = 4:4 = 1:1

Step 3: Since the ratio is 1:1, simply add all the quart amounts of all 4 ingredients to find the total amount of potting soil mixture.

$$4 + 3 + 2 + 2 = \mathbf{11}$$

2. (4) 6
Step 1: Find garden soil and peat moss in the *Ingredients* column. Find how many quarts of each are used in the potting soil mixture.

Step 2: Find the ratio of garden soil to peat moss.

   garden soil:peat moss = 4:3

Step 3: Set up a proportion to find the number of quarts of peat moss that corresponds to 8 quarts of garden soil.

$$\frac{4}{3} = \frac{8}{x}$$

Step 4: Find the cross product, and divide by the remaining term.

$$3 \times 8 = 24$$
$$24 \div 4 = \mathbf{6}$$

Tables and Charts

Directions: Choose the one best answer to each question.

Questions 1 through 3 refer to this table.

Median Household Income (Selected States)		
State	**1990**	**2000**
California	$35,798	$46,499
Florida	$27,483	$37,346
Illinois	$32,252	$45,606
Massachusetts	$36,952	$49,505
Texas	$27,016	$39,120

1. Which state had the lowest median household income in 1990?

(1) California
(2) Florida
(3) Illinois
(4) Massachusetts
(5) Texas

 2. Which state's median household income increased by the greatest amount from 1990 to 2000?

(1) California
(2) Florida
(3) Illinois
(4) Massachusetts
(5) Texas

 3. What was the difference in the median incomes of Massachusetts and Florida in 2000?

(1) $ 9,469
(2) $10,385
(3) $12,159
(4) $12,553
(5) $22,019

Questions 4 through 6 refer to this table.

2000 Earned Income Credit (EIC) Table				
Income from EIC worksheet		No Children	One Child	Two Children
At least	But less than			
$3000	3050	231	1029	1210
$3050	3100	235	1046	1230
$3100	3150	239	1063	1250
$3150	3200	243	1080	1270

4. George's income from the EIC worksheet was $3154 in 2000. According to the table, how much earned income credit will he receive if he has two children?

(1) $ 243
(2) $ 657
(3) $1080
(4) $1270
(5) $3200

 5. According to the table, how much more earned income credit will a person with one child and an income of $3000 receive than a person with no children and an income of $3000?

(1) $ 4
(2) $ 17
(3) $ 60
(4) $231
(5) $798

6. Velma had an income of $3050. According to the EIC worksheet, what is her earned income credit if she has one child?

(1) $1029
(2) $1046
(3) $1063
(4) $1080
(5) Not enough information is given.

Visitors to the Tourist Information Center	
Month	**Visitors**
May	2505
June	3650
July	4097
August	4162
September	2973

7. What was the total number of visitors for the months of June and July?

(1) 3650
(2) 4097
(3) 6155
(4) 7747
(5) 8229

Question 8 refers to this table.

Price Survey Results		
Store	**Detergent**	**Paper Towels**
EZ Shop	$5.99	$1.09
Gary's Grocery	$5.49	$0.99
B&C	$6.29	$0.99
Buy-1	$5.99	$1.09
Food-Fest	$6.09	$0.89
Two Rivers	$6.45	$1.09

8. Chen is taking a survey of prices of detergent and paper towels at local convenience stores. What is the difference in price between the most expensive and least expensive detergent?

(1) $0.10
(2) $0.30
(3) $0.36
(4) $0.50
(5) $0.96

Questions 9 and 10 refer to this table.

Nutrition Facts—Sunny Day Flakes		
Serving Size		$\frac{3}{4}$ cup
Servings per Container		8
Amount per Serving	Cereal	Cereal with $\frac{1}{2}$ cup skim milk
Calories	210	250
Fat Calories	40	40

9. How many cups of cereal are in the entire container of cereal?

(1) $\frac{3}{4}$
(2) 2
(3) $4\frac{1}{2}$
(4) 6
(5) 11

10. If Carrie eats three servings of cereal with milk during the week, how many total calories does she get from the three servings?

Mark your answer in the circles in the grid below.

> **TIP**
>
> When reading across a row in a table that has many columns, place a ruler or the edge of a piece of paper across the bottom of the row to read the data more accurately.

Answers and solutions start on page 114.

Data Analysis and Probability

Line Graphs

On the GED Mathematics Test, some problems may use a **line graph.** A line graph uses one or more lines to show how one quantity varies in relation to another. Most line graphs have a title that explains the information in the graph and labels that describe each **axis.** Some graphs have more than one line and a **key** that shows the meaning of each line.

The line graph below shows how the median weekly cost of living for a family of four increased from 1965 to 2000. To find the cost of living in 1970, look for 1970 on the bottom, or *x*-axis, of the graph. Find where the red line intersects the vertical line that is marked 1970. Look left to the horizontal side, or *y*-axis, of the graph. Find the label that shows the approximate cost of living in dollars for 1970. Since this point is about halfway between $100 and $150, the weekly cost of living for 1970 is about $125.

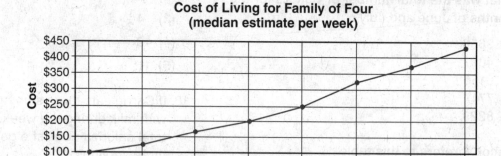

Cost of Living for Family of Four
(median estimate per week)

Use the line graph above to answer the two example questions below.

EXAMPLE 1: What was the cost of living for one week for a family of four in 1980?

STEP 1 Find 1980 on the x-axis. Follow the vertical line up to the point where it intersects the red line.

STEP 2 From the intersection, follow the horizontal line left to the *y*-axis. Read the number where the line intersects the *y*-axis.

ANSWER: $200

EXAMPLE 2: During which five-year period did the cost of living increase the most?

STEP 1 Find and estimate the cost of living amount for each year represented on the *x*-axis.

STEP 2 Subtract each year's cost of living from the cost during the following five-year period. For example, for 1965 to 1970: $125 – $100 = $25

1965 to 1970 = $25	1970 to 1975 = $45	1975 to 1980 = $30	1980 to 1985 = $50
1985 to 1990 = $75	1990 to 1995 = $45	1995 to 2000 = $55	

ANSWER: The greatest increase was from 1985 to 1990.

Practice the Skill

Try these examples. Choose the **one best answer** to each question. Then check your answers and the solutions.

Questions 1 and 2 refer to this line graph.

1. During which time period is production of containers the lowest?

    (1) 9–10
    (2) 10–11
    (3) 11–12
    (4) 12–1
    (5) 4–5

HINT Use the horizontal grid lines to help determine the lowest point on the red line.

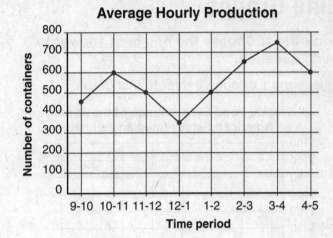

Average Hourly Production

2. What was the total number of containers produced from 9 to 12?

    (1) 1050
    (2) 1550
    (3) 1900
    (4) 2400
    (5) 3050

Calculator Hint: Some points will be between two axis lines. If the point appears to be halfway between two lines, estimate the value of the point by finding the average. Add the value of the two closest axis lines and then divide by two. To find the average of 400 and 500, key in: [(--- 400 + 500 ---)] ÷ 2 = The screen will display 450.

Answers and Solutions

1. (4) 12–1
Step 1: Find the point on the red line closest to the x-axis. This is the lowest point.

Step 2: Double check that there is no other point on the line closer to the x-axis.

Step 3: Follow that point straight down to the x-axis. Read the label for this line.

12–1

2. (2) 1550
Step 1: Find the number of containers produced during these three time periods: 9–10, 10–11, and 11–12. (Since the points for 9–10 and 11–12 appear to be halfway between two values, find the average of the two closest y-axis labels.)
$$9–10 = (500 + 400) ÷ 2 = 450$$
$$10–11 = 600$$
$$11–12 = 500$$

Step 2: Add the three numbers.
$$450 + 600 + 500 = \textbf{1550}$$

Line Graphs

Directions: Choose the <u>one best answer</u> to each question.

<u>Questions 1 through 3</u> refer to this graph.

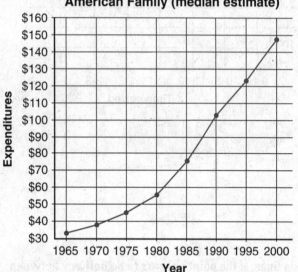

Weekly Food Expenditures of the Average American Family (median estimate)

1. What was the cost of the average American family's weekly food bill in 1985?

   (1) $103
   (2) $ 75
   (3) $ 55
   (4) $ 25
   (5) $ 7

2. During which five-year period did weekly food expenses increase the most?

   (1) 1965 to 1970
   (2) 1975 to 1980
   (3) 1985 to 1990
   (4) 1995 to 2000
   (5) Not enough information is given.

 3. By about what percent did food expenses increase between 1995 and 2000?

   (1) 10%
   (2) 21%
   (3) 35%
   (4) 79%
   (5) 125%

<u>Questions 4 through 6</u> refer to this graph.

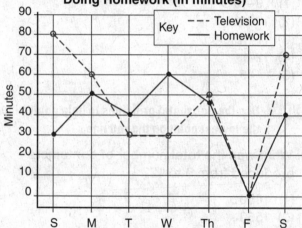

Time Watching Television and Doing Homework (in minutes)

4. For one week, Janice recorded the amount of time she spent watching television and doing homework. How much time did she spend doing homework that week?

   (1) 1 hour 50 minutes
   (2) 2 hours 20 minutes
   (3) 3 hours 45 minutes
   (4) 4 hours 25 minutes
   (5) Not enough information is given.

5. On which two days did Janice spend the same amount of time watching television?

   (1) Sunday and Monday
   (2) Monday and Tuesday
   (3) Monday and Saturday
   (4) Tuesday and Wednesday
   (5) Friday and Saturday

6. On which day did Janice spend more than twice the amount of time watching television as she spent doing homework?

   (1) Monday
   (2) Tuesday
   (3) Wednesday
   (4) Thursday
   (5) Sunday

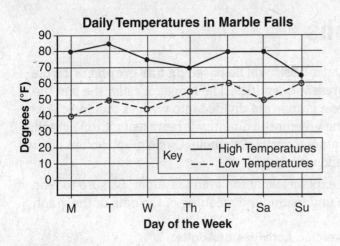

Daily Temperatures in Marble Falls

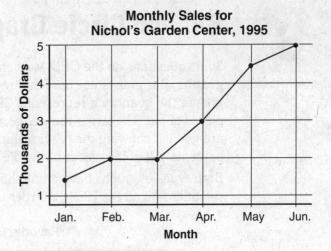

Monthly Sales for Nichol's Garden Center, 1995

7. What was the highest temperature recorded in Marble Falls during the week shown on the graph?

(1) 40°F
(2) 55°F
(3) 60°F
(4) 70°F
(5) 85°F

8. On which day did the greatest difference between the high temperature and the low temperature occur?

(1) Monday
(2) Tuesday
(3) Wednesday
(4) Friday
(5) Saturday

9. During which month(s) did sales exceed $4,000?

(1) January, February, and March
(2) January and June
(3) March, May, and June
(4) May and June
(5) June only

 10. What were the total sales for the first three months of the year?

(1) $ 1,500
(2) $ 5,500
(3) $12,500
(4) $18,000
(5) Not enough information is given.

 11. By what percent in decimal form did sales increase from March to May?

Mark your answer in the circles in the grid below.

	/	/	
.	.	.	.	.
0	0	0	0	0
1	1	1	1	1
2	2	2	2	2
3	3	3	3	3
4	4	4	4	4
5	5	5	5	5
6	6	6	6	6
7	7	7	7	7
8	8	8	8	8
9	9	9	9	9

[TIP]

Most line graphs on the GED Mathematics Tests show how units change over time. Time is usually on the x-axis (horizontal), and the unit that is changing is on the y-axis (vertical). Keep this in mind when reading line graphs.

Answers and solutions start on page 115.

Data Analysis and Probability

Bar and Circle Graphs

Some questions on the GED Mathematics Tests will be based on **bar graphs** or **circle graphs.** Bar graphs use bars that represent quantities. The longer or taller the bar, the greater the quantity it represents. Circle graphs are divided into wedges that look like pieces of pie. The larger the wedge, the greater the quantity it represents. Circle graphs are good at showing the relationship among parts of a whole. Circle graphs often involve percents. All of the pieces of the pie add up to 100%.

Both types of graphs have a title that explains what the graph is about. Be sure to read the titles and all the labels in order to understand the meaning of the data in the graph.

Favorite Exercise Activities of Adults

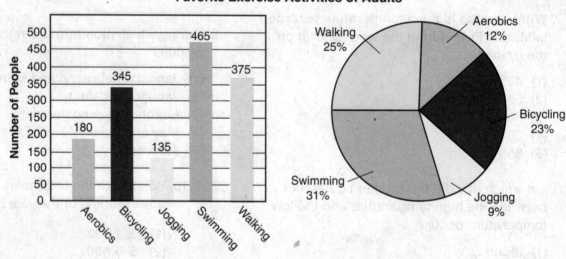

Use the graphs above to answer the example question below. Both graphs represent the same set of data.

EXAMPLE: How many more people surveyed prefer walking or jogging to swimming?

STEP 1 Choose the bar graph because it shows the actual number of people.

STEP 2 Add the number of people walking to the number of people jogging.

$$135 + 375 = 510$$

STEP 3 Subtract the number of people who prefer swimming from the total in Step 2.

$$510 - 465$$

ANSWER: 45 people

Practice the Skill

Try these examples. Choose the <u>one best answer</u> to each question. Then check your answers and the solutions.

<u>Questions 1 and 2</u> refer to the bar graph below.

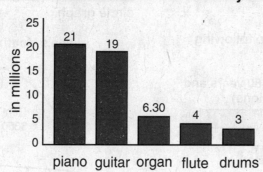

Instruments Americans Play

1. How many more millions of Americans play the piano than the organ?

    (1) 10
    (2) 14
    (3) 14.7
    (4) 21
    (5) 27.3

Calculator Hint: With decimal numbers, you do not need to enter leading or trailing zeros into your calculator. Enter 6.30 as 6.3. Enter 0.063 as .063. Enter 60.3 as 60.3.

2. How many millions of Americans play both the piano and the saxophone?

    (1) 4
    (2) 10
    (3) 21
    (4) 40
    (5) Not enough information is given.

HINT Find the bar for piano and for saxophone. Add their quantities together.

Answers and Solutions

1. (3) 14.7

Step 1: Find the quantities that correspond to the piano and organ bars.

    piano = 21   organ = 6.30

Step 2: Subtract the quantities.

    21 − 6.30 = **14.7**

2. (5) Not enough information is given.

Step 1: Find the quantities that correspond to the piano and saxophone bars.

    piano = 21   saxophone = no bar

Step 2: Since there is no bar, or data, for saxophones, you cannot answer the question.

Not enough information is given.

Bar and Circle Graphs

Directions: Choose the one best answer to each question.

Questions 1 through 3 refer to the following bar graph.

Population in the United States 80 years and older, 1960-2000 (in millions)

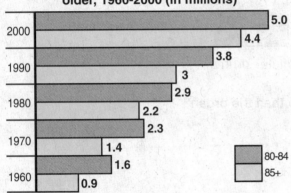

80-84
85+

1. What was the increase, in millions, in the population 85 and older from 1960 to 2000?

   (1) 0.7
   (2) 3.4
   (3) 3.5
   (4) 4.1
   (5) Not enough information is given.

2. When was the difference in the population of 80 to 84 year olds and the population of over 85 year olds the greatest?

   (1) 1950
   (2) 1960
   (3) 1970
   (4) 1980
   (5) 1990

3. By what percent did the population of 80 to 84 year olds increase from 1980 to 1990? Round to the nearest tenth of a percent.

   (1) 0.9%
   (2) 10%
   (3) 25.6%
   (4) 31%
   (5) 36.4%

Questions 4 through 6 refer to the following circle graph.

Lana's Monthly Budget for $1350

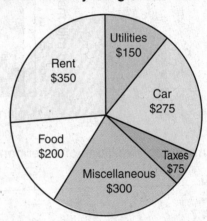

4. Approximately what percent of Lana's monthly income is spent on her car?

   (1) 5%
   (2) 11%
   (3) 16%
   (4) 20%
   (5) 45%

5. How many times more money does Lana spend on miscellaneous items than she spends on food?

   (1) 0.5
   (2) 1.5
   (3) 2
   (4) 15
   (5) 30

6. Which ratio compares the amount Lana spends on utilities to the amount she spends on rent?

   (1) $150 × $350
   (2) $150:$300
   (3) $\frac{150}{350}$
   (4) 2:1
   (5) Not enough information is given.

Questions 7 and 8 refer to the following bar graph.

Favorite Ways to Spend an Evening
(2100 people surveyed)

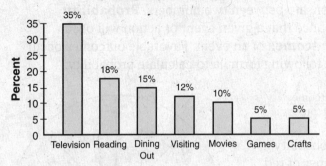

7. How many people chose watching television as their favorite way to spend an evening?

(1)   35
(2)   350
(3)   735
(4)   1735
(5)   3500

 8. How many more people chose reading than dining out?

Mark your answer in the circles in the grid below.

	⊘	⊘	⊘	
⊙	⊙	⊙	⊙	⊙
⓪	⓪	⓪	⓪	⓪
①	①	①	①	①
②	②	②	②	②
③	③	③	③	③
④	④	④	④	④
⑤	⑤	⑤	⑤	⑤
⑥	⑥	⑥	⑥	⑥
⑦	⑦	⑦	⑦	⑦
⑧	⑧	⑧	⑧	⑧
⑨	⑨	⑨	⑨	⑨

[TIP]

When you take the GED Mathematics Tests, if option (5) is "Not enough information is given," check the graph and the problem carefully to determine if there is adequate information to solve. If there is not enough information to solve, choose option (5).

Question 9 refers to the following circle graph.

Charlie's Activities in a 24-Hour Day

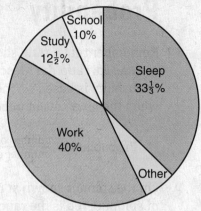

9. How can you determine the amount of hours Charlie spends in school in a day?

(1) Subtract 10% from 24, the number of hours in a day.
(2) Divide the number of hours in a day, 24, by 10%.
(3) Multiply 10% by 24, the number of hours in a day.
(4) Divide 10% by 24, the number of hours in a day.
(5) Not enough information is given.

Question 10 refers to the following circle graph.

Joe's Annual Car Expenses of $5000

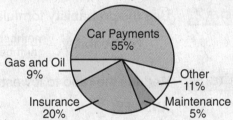

10. What is the ratio of the amount Joe spends for insurance to all other expenses combined?

(1) $\frac{1}{3}$

(2) $\frac{1}{4}$

(3) $\frac{1}{5}$

(4) $\frac{1}{6}$

(5) $\frac{1}{8}$

Answers and solutions start on page 115.

Skill 8: Bar and Circle Graphs **41**

Skill 9

Probability

Remember that a ratio shows a relationship between two numbers. **Probability** is a special ratio that describes the chance that a given event or action will occur. Probability is based on the possible **outcomes** of an event. Favorable outcomes occur when the given event occurs. Use the following formula to calculate probability:

$$\text{Probability} = \frac{\text{number of favorable outcomes}}{\text{number of possible outcomes}}$$

On the spinner shown at right, the probability of spinning red is the ratio of the number of red sections (3) to the total number of sections (8), or $\frac{3}{8}$. Since there are the same number of blue sections as red sections, the probability of the spinner landing on blue would also be $\frac{3}{8}$.

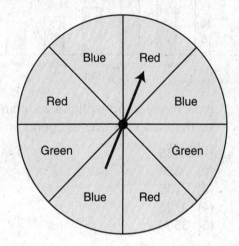

Use the spinner at right to answer the two example questions below.

EXAMPLE 1: What is the probability that the spinner will land on a green section?

STEP 1 Count the number of green sections (favorable outcomes) and the total number of sections (possible outcomes).

STEP 2 Use the probability formula to create a ratio.

$$\text{Probability} = \frac{\text{number of favorable outcomes}}{\text{number of possible outcomes}} = \frac{2}{8}$$

STEP 3 Reduce the ratio to lowest terms.

ANSWER: $\frac{1}{4}$

EXAMPLE 2: What is the probability of the spinner landing on a section that is not green?

STEP 1 Count the number of sections that are not green (favorable outcomes) and the total number of sections (possible outcomes).

STEP 2 Use the probability formula to create a ratio.

$$\text{Probability} = \frac{\text{number of favorable outcomes}}{\text{number of possible outcomes}} = \frac{6}{8}$$

STEP 3 Reduce the ratio to lowest terms.

ANSWER: $\frac{3}{4}$

Practice the Skill

Try these examples. Choose the <u>one best answer</u> to each question. Then check your answers and the solutions.

1. Carla bought 5 tickets for a prize drawing at the fair. If 200 tickets were sold, what is the probability that a ticket other than one of Carla's tickets will be drawn?

   (1) $\frac{1}{40}$

   (2) $\frac{5}{40}$

   (3) $\frac{39}{40}$

   (4) 5

   (5) 195

HINT What is the probability that Carla's ticket will <u>not</u> be drawn?

2. A jar holds 3 red marbles, 5 black marbles, 6 yellow marbles, and 4 green marbles. Rashad reaches into the jar without looking and selects a marble. What is the probability that the marble he selects is <u>not</u> yellow?

   (1) $\frac{1}{3}$

   (2) $\frac{2}{9}$

   (3) $\frac{2}{3}$

   (4) 6

   (5) 18

HINT What three colors will be favorable outcomes?

Answers and Solutions

1. (3) $\frac{39}{40}$

Step 1: Find the number of favorable outcomes (number of outcomes where Carla's ticket is *not* drawn) by subtracting the number of tickets she bought from the total number sold. The total number sold is the number of total outcomes.

   Favorable outcomes = 200 − 5 = 195
   Total outcomes = 200

Step 2: Use the probability formula.

   Probability = $\frac{195}{200}$

Step 3: Reduce the ratio to lowest terms by dividing the numerator and denominator by 5.

   $\frac{195}{200} \div \frac{5}{5} = \frac{39}{40}$

2. (3) $\frac{2}{3}$

Step 1: Find the number of favorable outcomes by adding to find the sum of the marbles that aren't yellow.

   Favorable outcomes = 3 + 5 + 4 = 12

Step 2: Then find the number of total outcomes by adding all marbles.

   Total outcomes = 3 + 5 + 6 + 4 = 18

Step 3: Use the probability formula.

   Probability = $\frac{12}{18}$

Step 4: Reduce the ratio to lowest terms by dividing the numerator and denominator by 6.

   $\frac{12}{18} \div \frac{6}{6} = \frac{2}{3}$

Probability

Directions: Choose the <u>one best answer</u> to each question.

<u>Questions 1 through 6</u> refer to the following spinner.

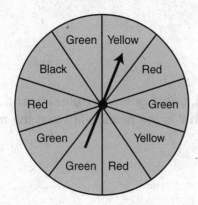

1. What is the probability of landing on black compared to landing on yellow?

   (1) $\frac{1}{3}$

   (2) $\frac{2}{1}$

   (3) $\frac{2}{10}$

   (4) $\frac{1}{2}$

   (5) $\frac{1}{10}$

 2. What is the probability of the spinner landing on yellow?

   (1) 2

   (2) $\frac{1}{3}$

   (3) $\frac{1}{4}$

   (4) $\frac{1}{5}$

   (5) $\frac{1}{10}$

3. What is the probability of the spinner landing on a section other than green?

   (1) 3

   (2) 6

   (3) $\frac{3}{5}$

   (4) $\frac{4}{5}$

   (5) $\frac{9}{10}$

4. What is the probability of the spinner landing on black?

   (1) $\frac{1}{10}$

   (2) $\frac{2}{10}$

   (3) $\frac{5}{10}$

   (4) $\frac{8}{10}$

   (5) $\frac{10}{10}$

5. Which expression can be used to find the probability of the spinner landing on a section other than red?

   (1) $\frac{3}{10}$

   (2) $\frac{10}{3}$

   (3) $\frac{(10-3)}{10}$

   (4) $\frac{(3-10)}{3}$

   (5) $\frac{(3+10)}{10}$

6. Which expression can be used to find the probability of the spinner landing on red or green?

   (1) $\frac{3}{10} + \frac{1}{10}$

   (2) $\frac{3}{10} + \frac{2}{10}$

   (3) $\frac{3}{10} + \frac{4}{10}$

   (4) $\frac{4}{10} - \frac{3}{10}$

   (5) $\frac{3}{10} + \frac{7}{10}$

> **TIP**
>
> A probability must always be equal to or less than 1. On the GED Mathematics Tests, eliminate any answer choices that are greater than 1 when asked to find a probability.

7. Van has 5 white socks, 4 blue socks, and 6 black socks in a drawer. If he pulls out one sock without looking, what is the probability that it will be a black sock?

Mark your answer in the circles in the grid below.

```
┌─┬─┬─┬─┬─┐
│ │/│/│/│ │
├─┼─┼─┼─┼─┤
│·│·│·│·│·│
├─┼─┼─┼─┼─┤
│0│0│0│0│0│
│1│1│1│1│1│
│2│2│2│2│2│
│3│3│3│3│3│
│4│4│4│4│4│
│5│5│5│5│5│
│6│6│6│6│6│
│7│7│7│7│7│
│8│8│8│8│8│
│9│9│9│9│9│
└─┴─┴─┴─┴─┘
```

8. On one school day at Juarez School, 45 students were wearing blue jeans, 125 students were wearing shorts, 80 students were wearing slacks, and some were wearing gym pants. What is the probability that a randomly selected student is wearing blue jeans?

(1) $\frac{1}{45}$

(2) $\frac{1}{250}$

(3) $\frac{9}{50}$

(4) $\frac{45}{50}$

(5) Not enough information is given.

Questions 9 through 11 refer to the following number cube.

A number cube has the numbers 1 through 6 on its faces.

9. What is the probability that the number 4 will be showing on top after the cube is tossed?

(1) 4

(2) $\frac{1}{5}$

(3) $\frac{1}{6}$

(4) $\frac{4}{6}$

(5) $\frac{6}{4}$

10. How do you calculate the probability that a 5 or a 6 will be showing on top after the number cube is tossed?

(1) Add the probability of rolling a 5 to the probability of rolling a 6.
(2) Multiply the probability of rolling a 5 by the probability of rolling a 6.
(3) Divide the probability of rolling a 6 by the probability of rolling a 5.
(4) Subtract the probability of rolling a 6 from the probability of rolling a 5.
(5) Not enough information is given.

11. What is the probability that an odd number will be showing on top after the cube is tossed?

(1) $\frac{1}{2}$

(2) $\frac{1}{3}$

(3) $\frac{1}{6}$

(4) $\frac{3}{4}$

(5) $\frac{5}{6}$

TIP

To find the probability of two independent events, find the probability of each event on its own. Then add the probabilities of each event.

Answers and solutions start on page 116.

Measurement and Geometry

Elapsed Time

On the GED Mathematics Tests, you may have to answer questions about **elapsed time.** Elapsed time is the amount of time that passes between a beginning time and an ending time. For example, between 6:00 and 8:00, two hours elapse. Two hours is the elapsed time.

You will need to know how to read an **analog clock.** An analog clock is a clock that displays the time of day by the position of two hands: a minute hand and an hour hand. The time on the analog clock is 6:30.

A **digital clock** is a clock that displays the time numerically. For example, the time on the analog clock above would be displayed with the numbers 6:30 on a digital clock.

If a time happens between midnight and noon (the morning), then you add A.M. after the time. If the time occurs between noon and midnight (the afternoon and night), you add P.M.

EXAMPLE: Pablo takes classes at a community college every day from 9:00 A.M. until 4:45 P.M. How much time passes between the end of Pablo's last class and the beginning of his first class the next day?

STEP 1 Determine the time span you want to find.

$$4:45 \text{ P.M. to } 9:00 \text{ A.M.} = ? \text{ hours}$$

STEP 2 Break the problem into easier problems.
Use midnight as a reference point.
There are 60 minutes in 1 hour, which means there are 15 minutes from 4:45 to 5:00. From 5:00 to midnight (12:00), there are 7 hours.

$$4:45 \text{ P.M. to midnight} = 7 \text{ hours } 15 \text{ minutes}$$
$$\text{midnight to } 9:00 \text{ A.M.} = 9 \text{ hours}$$

STEP 3 Add the time spans from the two smaller problems.

$$7 \text{ hours } 15 \text{ minutes} + 9 \text{ hours} = 16 \text{ hours } 15 \text{ minutes}$$

STEP 4 Convert the time span to a decimal by converting 15 minutes to hours.

$$15 \text{ minutes} \times \frac{1 \text{ hour}}{60 \text{ minutes}} = \frac{15 \text{ minutes}}{60 \text{ minutes}} = \frac{1}{4} = 0.25$$

STEP 5 Then add to 16 hours.

$$16 + 0.25 = 16.25$$

ANSWER: 16.25 hours

Practice the Skill

Try these examples. Choose the <u>one best answer</u> to each question. Then check your answers and the solutions.

1. Jeremiah plays with his community band every Tuesday at 5:30 P.M. If the clock at right shows the time that the band ends rehearsal every evening, how long are Jeremiah's rehearsals?

   (1) 1 hour 15 minutes
   (2) 1 hour 45 minutes
   (3) 2 hours 25 minutes
   (4) 2 hours 45 minutes
   (5) 3 hours 45 minutes

HINT Subtract the time in the question from the time on the clock.

Question 2 refers to this clock.

2. The time in Boston is shown on the clock above. If Sydney, Australia, is 14 hours ahead of Boston, what time is it in Sydney?

   (1) 11:00 P.M.
   (2) 11:00 A.M.
   (3)   1:00 P.M.
   (4)   1:00 A.M.
   (5)   3:00 P.M.

HINT If a time is described as *ahead*, add hours to the given time.

Answers and Solutions

1. (4) 2 hours 45 minutes

Step 1: Read the time on the clock–8:15 P.M.

Step 2: Subtract. Break the problem into smaller steps.

8:15 – 6:15 = 2 hours

6:15 – 5:30 = 45 minutes

    2 hours 45 minutes

2. (3) 1:00 P.M.

Step 1: Add 14 hours to 11:00 P.M.

Step 2: Break the problem into smaller parts. Remember that 12 hours later is the same time with a different label.

   11:00 P.M. + 12 hours = 11:00 A.M.

   11:00 A.M. + 1 hour = 12:00 P.M.

   12:00 P.M. + 1 hour = **1:00 P.M.**

Elapsed Time

Directions: Choose the <u>one best answer</u> to each question.

1. Sorin needs to take three busses to get to work every morning. He catches the first bus outside his house at 6:30 A.M. He is dropped off at 6:54 A.M. to wait for the second bus, which picks him up at 7:08 A.M. The second bus drops him off at 7:31 A.M. The third bus picks him up at 7:40 A.M. and drops him off at work at 7:52 A.M. How many minutes does Sorin spend waiting for the connecting busses?

   (1) 61
   (2) 38
   (3) 35
   (4) 28
   (5) 23

Question 2 refers to this clock.

2. Emelda is cooking lasagna for dinner. The recipe says to cook the dish at 350°F for 1 hour 20 minutes. The clock above represents the time she took the lasagna out of the oven. What time did she put the lasagna in the oven?

   (1) 5:15
   (2) 5:20
   (3) 5:30
   (4) 6:20
   (5) 6:40

3. Sam has been training for a marathon, which is 26.2 miles. He has found that he can run that distance in about 4 hours 25 minutes. The day of the race, Sam's starting time is 9:00 A.M. What time will Sam most likely finish the race?

   (1) 12:25 P.M.
   (2) 1:25 P.M.
   (3) 2:25 P.M.
   (4) 12:25 A.M.
   (5) 1:25 A.M.

4. The hometown baseball team was rained out last night, so today they are playing two games. The first game starts at 1:00 P.M. If the game ends at 3:45 P.M. and there is a rest period of 1 hour 10 minutes between games, what time does the second game start?

   (1) 4:55 A.M.
   (2) 4:50 P.M.
   (3) 4:55 P.M.
   (4) 5:05 P.M.
   (5) Not enough information is given.

Question 5 refers to these clocks.

5. How much time elapsed between the time on the left to the time on the right?

   (1) 4 hours 25 minutes
   (2) 6 hours 25 minutes
   (3) 6 hours 35 minutes
   (4) 7 hours 25 minutes
   (5) 7 hours 35 minutes

6. Tyree can process 30 orders per hour. This morning he arrived at work at 8:30 A.M. and has 90 orders to process. What time will Tyree finish processing those orders?

(1) 11:30 A.M.
(2) 11:00 A.M.
(3) 10:30 A.M.
(4) 10:30 P.M.
(5) 11:30 P.M.

7. Jaime planned a long hike in the White Mountains for Saturday. He wanted to start at the trail head very early in the morning to avoid the summer heat and the crowds. He went to bed at 9:45 P.M. the night before and slept until 5:15 A.M. on Saturday morning. For how many hours did Jaime sleep?

Mark your answer in the circles in the grid below.

Question 8 refers to this figure.

8. Jennifer takes a 35-minute lunch break at her job every day. Her break started at 1:00 P.M. today. On the clock above, to which number will the minute hand point when her lunch break is over?

(1) 3
(2) 4
(3) 5
(4) 6
(5) 7

9. The time in Denver is 2 hours behind the time in Washington, D.C. The distance between the two cities is 1442 miles. A plane leaves Denver at 11:20 A.M. and arrives in Washington, D.C. at 5:05 P.M. local time. How long was the flight?

(1) 2 hours
(2) 2 hours 45 minutes
(3) 3 hours 45 minutes
(4) 5 hours 45 minutes
(5) 6 hours 15 minutes

TIP

To read an analog clock correctly, remember to first look at the shorter hand to determine the hour. Then look at the longer hand to find the minute. Since analog clocks do not show whether the time is A.M. or P.M., read the problem carefully to find context to determine the correct time of day.

Answers and solutions start on page 117.

KEY Skill 11

Lines and Angles

Some questions on the GED Mathematics Tests will be based on **lines** and **angles**. A line is a never-ending path that can be drawn through two **points**. Angles exist in many varieties. Look at the types of angles and lines below. The letter m before an angle sign ($\angle$) means "the measure of."

Perpendicular Lines

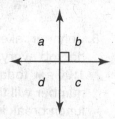

All angles are equal to 90°.
$m\angle a = m\angle b = m\angle c = m\angle d = 90°$

Complementary Angles

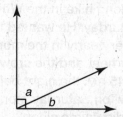

The sum of the angles is 90°.
$m\angle a + m\angle b = 90°$

Supplementary Angles

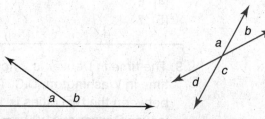

The sum of the angles is 180°.
$m\angle a + m\angle b = 180°$

Vertical Angles

Vertical (opposite) angles are congruent. Congruent angles have the same size and measure.
$m\angle a = m\angle c$ and $m\angle b = m\angle d$

Parallel Lines Cut by a Transversal

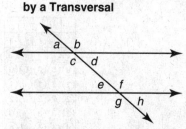

Alternate exterior angles are equal.
$m\angle a = m\angle h$ and $m\angle b = m\angle g$
Alternate interior angles are equal.
$m\angle c = m\angle f$ and $m\angle d = m\angle e$

EXAMPLE: The ratio of two supplementary angles is 4:5. What is the measure of the larger angle?

STEP 1 Recognize that supplementary angles add to 180°.

$$\angle A + \angle B = 180°$$

STEP 2 Set up an expression. Four times a number plus five times the same number equals 180°. Let $4x = \angle A$ and $5x = \angle B$.

$$4x + 5x = 180°$$

STEP 3 Solve for x.

$$9x = 180°, x = \frac{180°}{9} = 20°$$

STEP 4 Find $m\angle A$ and $m\angle B$ by substituting in the value of x. Choose the larger angle.

$$\angle A = 4x = 4(20°) = 80°$$

$$\angle B = 5x = 5(20°) = 100°$$

ANSWER: $m\angle B = 100°$

Practice the Skill

Try these examples. Choose the one best answer to each question. Then check your answers and the solutions.

Questions 1 and 2 refer to the figure below.

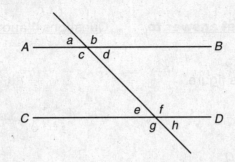

1. $\overline{AB}$ is parallel to $\overline{CD}$. Which of the following statements is true?

   (1) $m\angle a + m\angle b = 90°$
   (2) $m\angle a + m\angle e = 180°$
   (3) $m\angle a = m\angle g$
   (4) $m\angle a = m\angle d$
   (5) $m\angle a + m\angle d = 180°$

   HINT Look for supplementary pairs of angles and vertical (opposite) angles.

2. If $m\angle c = 135°$, what is the measure of $\angle d$?

   (1) 15°
   (2) 30°
   (3) 45°
   (4) 60°
   (5) 135°

    Calculator Hint: When adding or subtracting angle measures with your calculator, temporarily ignore the degree sign and just enter the numbers. Since $\angle c$ and $\angle d$ are supplementary angles, what is the measure of $\angle d$? Use your calculator to solve.

Answers and Solutions

1. (4) $m\angle a = m\angle d$
Look at each answer choice and determine if it is true.

(1) $\angle a$ and $\angle b$ are supplementary (180°), not complementary.
(2) $m\angle a$ and $m\angle e$ are equal, but since they are both less than 90°, they will not add to 180°.
(3) Angles a and g are supplementary because $m\angle c = m\angle g$, and angles a and c are supplementary but not equal.
(4) $m\angle a = m\angle d$ because the angles are opposite and congruent.
(5) $m\angle a$ and $m\angle d$ are opposite and equal, but not supplementary.
$$m\angle a = m\angle d$$

2. (3) 45°
Step 1: Find a relationship between $\angle c$ and $\angle d$. The angles are supplementary because they exist on one line that is only intersected by one other line. The measure of the sum of a pair of supplementary angles is 180°.

Step 2: Write an expression for the relationship.
$$m\angle c + m\angle d = 180°$$

Step 3: Substitute for $m\angle c$ and solve.
$$135° + m\angle d = 180°$$
$$m\angle d = 180° - 135°$$
$$m\angle d = \mathbf{45°}$$

Lines and Angles

Directions: Choose the <u>one best answer</u> to each question.

<u>Questions 1 through 3</u> refer to this figure.

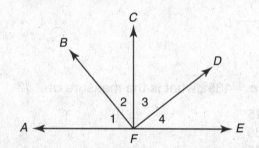

1. ∠AFB and ∠BFC are complementary angles. If m∠AFB = 50°, which expression could be used to find the measure of ∠BFC?

   (1) 180° − 50°
   (2) 90° + 50°
   (3) 90° − 50°
   (4) 180° ÷ 50°
   (5) 90°(50°)

 2. What is m∠2 if m∠4 = 37.6°?

   (1) 45°
   (2) 52.4°
   (3) 90°
   (4) 127.6°
   (5) Not enough information is given.

3. If m∠CFE is 90°, which of the following expressions represents the measure of m∠CFA?

   (1) 90° + 90°
   (2) 90° − 45°
   (3) 180° ÷ 90°
   (4) 180° − 90°
   (5) 180° + 90°

<u>Questions 4 and 5</u> refer to this figure.

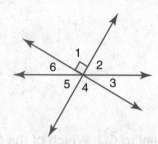

4. Which of the following statements about the angles in the figure above is true?

   (1) m∠2 and m∠3 add to 180°.
   (2) m∠1 plus m∠4 equals 90°.
   (3) m∠1 and m∠2 add to 90°.
   (4) m∠5 and m∠6 are equal and opposite.
   (5) m∠6 and m∠3 add to 180°.

5. Acute angles are angles that measure less than 90°. How many acute angles are in the figure?

   Mark your answer in the circles in the grid below.

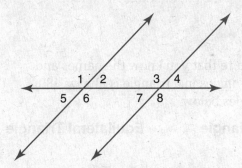

6. Why do ∠1 and ∠6 have equal measures?

(1) They are beside each other.
(2) They are complementary angles.
(3) They are supplementary angles.
(4) They are vertical, or opposite, angles.
(5) They are on opposite sides of the transversal.

7. In the figure above, the two lines that intersect the horizontal line are parallel. Which of the following angle pairs have the same angle measure?

(1) ∠5 and ∠1
(2) ∠5 and ∠2
(3) ∠5 and ∠4
(4) ∠5 and ∠6
(5) ∠5 and ∠8

 8. If the lines are parallel and m∠2 is 45° in the figure above, what is the measure of ∠3?

(1) 30°
(2) 45°
(3) 90°
(4) 135°
(5) 180°

 9. The sum of two angles equals 90°. The ratio of the two angles is 7:8. What is the measure of the larger angle?

(1) 6°
(2) 42°
(3) 48°
(4) 84°
(5) Not enough information is given.

Question 10 refers to this figure.

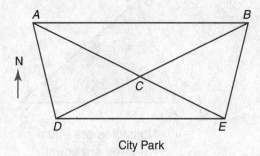

City Park

10. The drawing of City Park above shows two diagonal paths that cross at point C in the center of the park. If m∠DAB = m∠EBA and m∠DCE = 105°, what is the measure of ∠ACB?

(1) 15°
(2) 75°
(3) 105°
(4) 135°
(5) 180°

TIP

When finding the relationships among angles, such as equal angles, opposite angles, angles that add to 180°, and angles that add to 90°, write the measures of the angles on the diagram. If you don't know any of the measurements, create your own symbols to show which angles are equal.

Answers and solutions start on page 117.

KEY Skill 12

Triangles

Some items on the GED Mathematics Tests require that you know the names and properties of certain **triangles.** The sum of the angles in a triangle is always 180°. Look at the characteristics of the types of triangles below.

Scalene Triangle

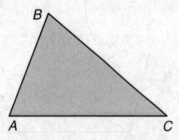

No angles are equal.
No sides are equal.

Isosceles Triangle

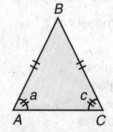

Two angles are equal.
Two sides are equal.

$m\angle a = m\angle c$
$AB = CB$

Equilateral Triangle

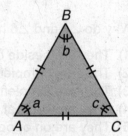

All angles are equal.
All sides are equal.

Right Triangle

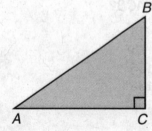

One angle is 90°.
The side opposite the 90° angle is the largest side.
$m\angle c = 90°$

Acute Triangle

All angles are
less than 90°.

Obtuse Triangle

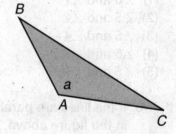

One angle is
greater than 90°.
$m\angle a > 90°$

EXAMPLE: What are the measures of the angles in an equilateral triangle?

STEP 1 Recall the characteristics of an equilateral triangle—an equilateral triangle has equal sides and angles.

STEP 2 Recall that the sum of the measures of the angles of a triangle is 180°. Divide by the number of angles (3).

$$180° \div 3 = 60°$$

ANSWER: 60°

Practice the Skill

Try these examples. Choose the one best answer to each question. Then check your answers and the solutions.

Question 1 refers to the figure below.

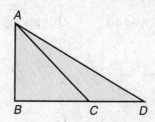

1. In the figure above, triangle *ABC* is an isosceles right triangle. What are the measures of its three angles?

    (1) 30°, 60°, 90°
    (2) 45°, 45°, 90°
    (3) 60°, 60°, 60°
    (4) 60°, 90°, 60°
    (5) Not enough information is given.

HINT What are the characteristics of an isosceles triangle?

2. Two angles of a triangle measure 36° and 44°. Which expression below could be used to find the measure of the third angle?

    (1) 36 + 44 + 180
    (2) 36 + (44 − 180)
    (3) 180 − (36 + 44)
    (4) 180 − (36 − 44)
    (5) 90 − 36 − 44

 Calculator Hint: Numbers can be added in any order: 3 + 4 = 4 + 3. However, numbers cannot be subtracted in any order: 4 − 3 ≠ 3 − 4. When you enter numbers into your calculator, make sure to enter them in the correct order.

Answers and Solutions

1. (2) 45°, 45°, 90°
Step 1: Recall the characteristics of an isosceles right triangle:
 - Interior angles add to 180°.
 - Two angles are equal.
 - One angle is a right angle (90°).

Step 2: Choose the answer choice that includes all the characteristics named in Step 1.

    45°, 45°, 90°

2. (3) 180 − (36 + 44)
Step 1: Recall that the sum of a triangle's interior angles is 180°.

Step 2: Write an equation to represent the sum of the interior angles. Let *x* = the third angle.

    36° + 44° + x = 180°

Step 3: Solve for *x*.

    x = 180 − (36 + 44)

Triangles

Directions: Choose the <u>one best answer</u> to each question.

Questions 1 through 3 refer to this figure.

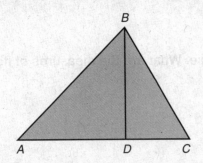

1. Triangle *ABC* is divided into two triangles. If $\overline{BD}$ is perpendicular to $\overline{AC}$, which of the following must be true?

   (1) Triangle *ABC* is a right triangle.
   (2) Triangle *BCD* is an acute triangle.
   (3) Triangle *ABD* is an obtuse triangle.
   (4) Triangle *ADB* is a right triangle.
   (5) Triangle *BDC* is an isosceles triangle.

2. If $\overline{BD}$ is perpendicular to $\overline{AC}$, how many right triangles are in the figure?

   (1) 1
   (2) 2
   (3) 3
   (4) 4
   (5) 5

 3. If triangle *ADB* has two angles with the same measure and the measure of $\angle ADB = 90°$, what is the measure of $\angle A$?

   (1) 30°
   (2) 45°
   (3) 60°
   (4) 90°
   (5) Not enough information is given.

Questions 4 through 6 refer to this figure.

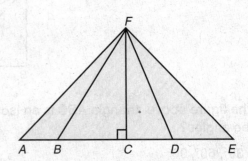

4. Which of the following are obtuse triangles?

   (1) *AFB* and *AFC*
   (2) *AFC* and *EFB*
   (3) *DFC* and *BEF*
   (4) *EFD* and *AFB*
   (5) *AFE* and *AFC*

 5. Angle *FAE* and angle *FEA* have equal measures. The measure of $\angle AFE = 96°$. What is the measure of $\angle FEA$?

   Mark your answer in the circles in the grid below.

6. How many triangles are there in the figure above?

   (1) 4
   (2) 5
   (3) 7
   (4) 8
   (5) 10

Question 7 refers to this figure.

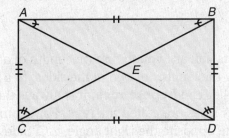

7. An isosceles triangle has two equal sides and two equal angles. How many isosceles triangles are in rectangle *ABCD*?

   (1) 1
   (2) 2
   (3) 3
   (4) 4
   (5) 5

Question 8 refers to this figure.

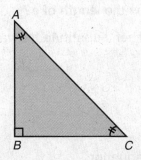

8. Triangle *ABC* has two equal angles. If *m∠B* = 90°, which of the following could be used to find the measure of *∠A*?

   (1) 180° − 90°

   (2) $\frac{(180° - 90°)}{2}$

   (3) $\frac{(180° + 90°)}{2}$

   (4) 2(90°)

   (5) $\frac{180°}{2}$

Questions 9 through 11 refer to this figure.

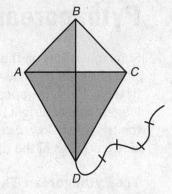

9. The perpendicular cross-pieces on the kite divide the kite into four triangles. What kind of triangles are they?

   (1) right
   (2) obtuse
   (3) acute
   (4) scalene
   (5) equilateral

10. $\overline{AD}$ is congruent to $\overline{CD}$. If *m∠CAD* is 55°, what is the measure of *∠ADC*?

   (1) 60°
   (2) 70°
   (3) 90°
   (4) 110°
   (5) 180°

11. *m∠BAC* = *m∠BCA*. If $\overline{AB}$ = 12 inches, how long is $\overline{CB}$ in inches?

   (1) 8
   (2) 10
   (3) 12
   (4) 36
   (5) 90

> **TIP**
>
> The sum of the angles of every triangle is 180°. If you know the measure of two angles, subtract them from 180° to find the measure of the third angle.

Answers and solutions start on page 118.

Skill 13

Pythagorean Theorem

Some questions on the GED Mathematics Tests will ask you to find the length of a third side of a right triangle when you already know the lengths of two of the sides. In a right triangle, the side opposite the right angle is called the **hypotenuse.** It is always the longest side of a right triangle. The two shorter sides are called the **legs.** For example, in the triangle below, c is the hypotenuse, the side opposite the right angle, $\angle C$. Side a and side b are legs of the right triangle.

The **Pythagorean Theorem** states that the sum of the squares of both legs is equal to the square of the hypotenuse. The Pythagorean Theorem is represented by the formula $a^2 + b^2 = c^2$. This is called the **Pythagorean relationship.**

Use the triangle at right to answer the two example questions below.

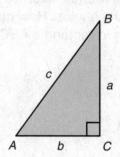

EXAMPLE 1: If $a = 8$ inches and $b = 6$ inches, what is the length of c?

STEP 1 Write the equation for the Pythagorean Theorem. Then substitute the values for a and b.

$$a^2 + b^2 = c^2$$
$$8^2 + 6^2 = c^2$$

STEP 2 Calculate the squares.

$$64 + 36 = c^2$$

STEP 3 Add and take the square root of both sides of the equation.

$$\sqrt{100} = \sqrt{c^2}$$

ANSWER: $c = 10$

EXAMPLE 2: If $b = 9$ inches and $c = 15$ inches, what is the length of a?

STEP 1 Write the equation for the Pythagorean Theorem. Then substitute the values for b and c.

$$a^2 + b^2 = c^2$$
$$a^2 + 9^2 = 15^2$$

STEP 2 Calculate the squares.

$$a^2 + 81 = 225$$

STEP 3 Subtract 81 from each side. Then find the square root of both sides of the equation.

$$a^2 = 225 - 81 = 144$$
$$\sqrt{a^2} = \sqrt{144}$$

ANSWER: $a = 12$ inches

Practice the Skill

Try these examples. Choose the <u>one best answer</u> to each question. Then check your answers and the solutions.

<u>Questions 1 and 2</u> refer to the figure at right.

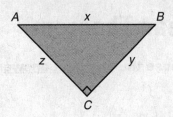

1. Triangle *ACB* is an isosceles right triangle. It has one right angle and two angles of equal measure. Which of the following equations can be used to represent the value of *x*?

(1) $x = \sqrt{2y^2}$

(2) $x = \sqrt{4y^2}$

(3) $x = 4y^2$

(4) $x^2 = y^2$

(5) $x^2 = 2y^4$

HINT Determine which two sides are equal, and then substitute so that there are only two variables.

2. In isosceles right triangle *ACB* above, if *x* = 4, what is the length of *y*?

(1) $\sqrt{2}$

(2) $\sqrt{4}$

(3) $\sqrt{8}$

(4) $\sqrt{10}$

(5) Not enough information is given.

 Calculator Hint: Use your calculator to find square roots. To find the square root of 81, key in:

81 [SHIFT] [$\sqrt{}$ x^2]

Answers and Solutions

1. (1) $x = \sqrt{2y^2}$
Step 1: The triangle has two equal sides. Write an equation for the two equal sides.
$$y = z$$

Step 2: Write the equation for the Pythagorean Theorem.
$$z^2 + y^2 = x^2$$

Step 3: Substitute for *z*.
$$y^2 + y^2 = x^2$$

Step 4: Add and solve for *x*.
$$x^2 = 2y^2$$
$$x = \sqrt{2y^2}$$

2. (3) $\sqrt{8}$
Step 1: Write the equation for the Pythagorean Theorem.
$$z^2 + y^2 = x^2$$

Step 2: Substitute for *z* and *x* (remember *z* = *y*). Then add and calculate the square.
$$y^2 + y^2 = 4^2$$
$$2y^2 = 16$$

Step 3: Divide and solve for *y*.
$$y^2 = 8$$
$$y = \sqrt{8}$$

Pythagorean Theorem

Directions: Choose the <u>one best answer</u> to each question.

<u>Questions 1 through 3</u> refer to this figure.

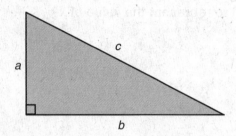

1. In the figure above, if $a = 7$ centimeters and $b = 10$ centimeters, which of the following expressions could be used to find c?

   (1) $\sqrt{10^2 - 7^2}$
   (2) $\sqrt{7^2 - 10^2}$
   (3) $\sqrt{7^2 - 10^2}$
   (4) $\sqrt{7^2 + 10^2}$
   (5) $\sqrt{7 + 10}$

 2. In the figure above, if $c = 26$ feet and $b = 24$ feet, what is the length, in feet, of a?

   (1) 5
   (2) 10
   (3) 12
   (4) 35
   (5) 50

3. In the figure above, if $a = 1$ meter and $c = 3$ meters, the length of b, in meters, will fall between which two whole numbers?

   (1) 1 and 2
   (2) 2 and 3
   (3) 3 and 4
   (4) 4 and 5
   (5) 5 and 6

<u>Questions 4 and 5</u> refer to this figure.

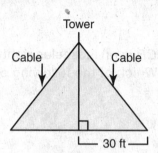

 4. In the figure above, the radio tower is perpendicular to the ground. How many feet long must the support cables be if they are attached 5 feet below the top of the tower and are anchored to the ground?

   (1) 36
   (2) 40
   (3) 46
   (4) 48
   (5) Not enough information is given.

5. If the height of the tower is 45 feet, how long, in feet, must the support cables be?

   (1) 36
   (2) 40
   (3) 46
   (4) 48
   (5) 50

> **TIP**
>
> Don't assume that a triangle is a right triangle because it looks like a right triangle. Read the question to see if the angle measure is given, or find evidence in the figure, such as the right angle symbol, or find the measures of the other two angles to prove that the third angle is 90°.

Question 6 refers to this figure.

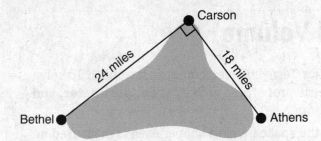

 6. How would you determine how far across the lake it is from Bethel to Athens?

(1) Use the Pythagorean Theorem. Let $c = 24$ miles and $b = 18$ for the sides. Solve for a.

(2) Use the law of squares. Let $a = 24$ miles and $b = 18$ miles. Solve for c.

(3) Use the Pythagorean Theorem. Let $a = 24$ miles and $b = 18$ miles. Solve for c.

(4) Use a ruler to measure the distance on paper.

(5) Not enough information is given.

Question 7 refers to this figure.

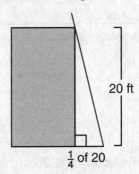

20 ft

$\frac{1}{4}$ of 20

7. A ladder is leaning against a two-story building. Because of safety regulations, the ladder must be placed so that the distance from the bottom of the ladder to the building is $\frac{1}{4}$ of the height of the building. The ladder also must extend 3 feet above the building. Which expression can be used to determine how many feet long the ladder must be to meet these requirements?

(1) $20 + 3$

(2) $\sqrt{400} - \sqrt{25} + 3$

(3) $\sqrt{425}$

(4) $\sqrt{425} + 3$

(5) $20 - 5 + 3$

Question 8 refers to this figure.

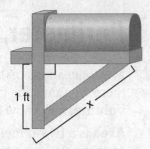

1 ft

x

 8. The figure above shows the side view of plans for a post used for mailboxes. The post extends 1 foot below the cross support. If the mailbox is 16 inches long, how many inches long is the brace?

Mark your answer in the circles in the grid below.

Question 9 refers to this figure.

Gate A   Gate B

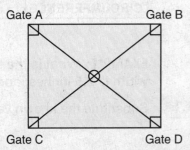

Gate C   Gate D

 9. The paths in North Park, shown above, intersect in the center of the park. From Gate A to the center is 25 yards. From Gate A to Gate C is 30 yards. How far is it in yards from Gate A to Gate B?

(1) 40

(2) 45

(3) 60

(4) 75

(5) 100

Answers and solutions start on page 118.

Skill 14

Perimeter, Area, and Volume

Many questions on the GED Mathematics Tests involve geometric formulas. To solve them, you must be familiar with geometric properties, such as **area, perimeter,** and **volume,** and know how to solve for them.

Area is a two-dimensional measure of the space inside a shape. Area is measured in square units, such as square feet, square inches, or square meters.

Perimeter is the distance around the outside of a two-dimensional shape. Perimeter is measured in one-dimensional units, such as feet, inches, and meters.

Circumference is a special name for the perimeter of a circle.

Volume is a three-dimensional measure of the space inside a solid figure. Volume is measured in three-dimensional units, such as cubic inches, cubic feet, or cubic meters.

Formulas will be provided to you on test day, but you should be familiar with those listed below so that you can use them quickly and easily.

AREA of a:		**VOLUME** of a:	
square	$= side^2$	cube	$= edge^3$
rectangle	$= length \times width$	rectangular solid	$= length \times width \times height$
parallelogram	$= base \times height$	square pyramid	$= \frac{1}{3} \times (base\ edge)^2 \times height$
triangle	$= \frac{1}{2} \times base \times height$	cylinder	$= \pi \times radius^2 \times height$
trapezoid	$= \frac{1}{2} \times (base_1 + base_2) \times height$	cone	$= \frac{1}{3} \times \pi \times radius^2 \times height$
circle	$= \pi \times radius^2$		

PERIMETER of a:

square	$= 4 \times side$
rectangle	$= 2 \times length + 2 \times width$
triangle	$= side_1 + side_2 + side_3$

CIRCUMFERENCE of a circle $= \pi \times diameter$

π is approximately equal to 3.14.

EXAMPLE: What is the height of a box in inches if the volume is 30 cubic inches, the width is 2.5 inches, and the length is 3 inches?

STEP 1 Substitute the known values into the formula for the volume of a box (rectangular solid).

$$volume = length \times width \times height$$
$$30 \text{ in.}^3 = 3 \text{ in.} \times 2.5 \text{ in.} \times height$$

STEP 2 Simplify and solve for the unknown variable.

$$30 \text{ in.}^3 = 7.5 \text{ in.}^2 \times height$$
$$height = 30 \text{ in.}^3 \div 7.5 \text{ in.}^2 = 4 \text{ in.}$$

ANSWER: height = 4 inches

Practice the Skill

Try these examples. Choose the <u>one best answer</u> to each question. Then check your answers and the solutions.

1. A cardboard box measures $1\frac{1}{2}$ feet on each edge. Which expression below represents the volume of the box?

   (1) $\left(1\frac{1}{2}\right)^2$

   (2) $3\left(1\frac{1}{2}\right)$

   (3) $4\left(1\frac{1}{2}\right)$

   (4) $\left(1\frac{1}{2}\right)^3$

   (5) $4\left(1\frac{1}{2}\right)^3$

 Calculator Hint: Use $\boxed{x^2}$ to find a number raised to the power of 2, and use $\boxed{}$ $\boxed{\blacktriangleright}$ to find a number raised to the power of 3.

2. One side of a roof has an area of 1,953 square feet. The height of the house is shown. What is the length of the roof?

   (1) 21 feet
   (2) 63 feet
   (3) 93 feet
   (4) 114 feet
   (5) Not enough information is given.

21 ft

HINT Use the formula for the area of a rectangle, and solve for the width.

Answers and Solutions

1. (4) $\left(1\frac{1}{2}\right)^3$

Step 1: Choose the appropriate formula.
  volume = length × width × height

Step 2: Substitute the known values.
  volume = $1\frac{1}{2} \times 1\frac{1}{2} \times 1\frac{1}{2}$

Step 3: Simplify and solve for the unknown variable.
  volume = $\left(1\frac{1}{2}\right)^3$

2. (5) Not enough information is given.

Step 1: Choose the appropriate formula.
  area of rectangle = length × width

Step 2: Substitute the known values.
  1,953 ft² = length × width

Step 3: The height of the house is given, but is not applicable to the problem. There are two unknown variables, so **not enough information is given** in the question to solve the problem.

Perimeter, Area, and Volume

Directions: Choose the <u>one best answer</u> to each question.

1. Which of the following expressions represents the distance around a 9' × 12' carpet?

   (1) 9 + 12
   (2) 9 × 12
   (3) 2(9) + 2(12)
   (4) 122 + 92
   (5) 4(9) × 12

 2. How many cubic feet of concrete will you need to make a walkway that is 15 feet by 3 feet by 6 inches?

   (1) 15
   (2) 22.5
   (3) 45
   (4) 90
   (5) 270

<u>Question 3</u> refers to this figure.

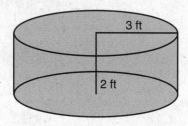

3. A child's swimming pool has an inside radius of 3 feet and an inside height of 2 feet. Which expression can be used to find its volume?

   (1) 3.14(9)(2)
   (2) 3.14(6)(2
   (3) 3.14(3)(2)
   (4) 3.14(32)
   (5) Not enough information is given.

 4. A square quilt is made of 36 twelve-inch squares. What are the dimensions of the quilt in feet?

   (1) 3 × 12
   (2) 4 × 9
   (3) 6 × 6
   (4) 6 × 4
   (5) 12 × 12

<u>Question 5</u> refers to this figure.

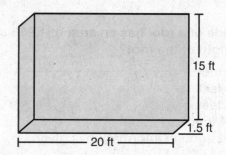

5. A rectangular patio is being made out of concrete. The patio will be 20 feet long by 15 feet wide. If concrete is to be poured to a depth of 1.5 feet, which expression can be used to find the number of cubic yards of concrete that is needed? (1 cubic yard = 27 cubic feet)

   (1) (20)(15) ÷ 27
   (2) 20 + 15 + 1.5 × 27
   (3) (20)(15)(1.5) ÷ 3
   (4) (20)(15)(1.5)(27)
   (5) (20)(15)(1.5) ÷ 27

 6. A large circular flower bed has a diameter of 6 yards. How many yards of fencing are needed to enclose the garden?

   (1)   0.42
   (2)   0.84
   (3) 18.84
   (4) 36
   (5) 113.04

Questions 7 and 8 refer to this figure.

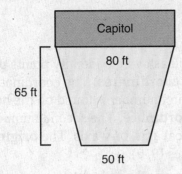

Capitol

80 ft

65 ft

50 ft

7. The lawn in front of the Capitol building is in the shape of a trapezoid. Use the diagram to find the area of the lawn in square feet.

   (1) 1950
   (2) 3250
   (3) 4000
   (4) 4225
   (5) 8450

8. If you wanted to find the total area of the Capitol and its lawn, which of the following expressions should you use? The width of the Capitol is 32 feet.

   (1) $\frac{1}{2} \times (50 \times 80) \times 65 + (32 + 80)$

   (2) $\frac{1}{2} \times (50 + 80) \times 65 + (32 \times 80)$

   (3) $\frac{1}{2} \times 80 \times 65 + (32 \times 80)$

   (4) $\frac{1}{2} \times 50 \times 65 + (32 \times 80)$

   (5) $\frac{1}{2} \times (50 + 80) + (32 \times 80)$

9. How many 12-inch square tiles are needed to completely cover the floor of a greenhouse that is 25 feet by 40 feet?

   (1) 12,000
   (2) 1,000
   (3)   100
   (4)   83
   (5)   65

TIP

Convert all the measurements in a problem to the same unit before you perform any calculations.

10. A rectangular fish pond holds 30 cubic feet of water. What is the depth of the pond if it is 8 feet long and 5 feet wide?

    (1) 75 inches
    (2) 40 inches
    (3) 9 inches
    (4) 7.5 inches
    (5) 3 inches

Questions 11 and 12 refer to this figure.

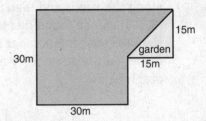

30m

15m

garden

15m

30m

11. What is the perimeter, in meters, of the backyard and garden shown in the drawing?

    (1)   90
    (2) 135
    (3) 150
    (4) 600
    (5) Not enough information is given.

12. What is the area in square meters of the triangular garden shown in the drawing above?

    Mark your answer in the circles in the grid below.

Measurement and Geometry

Skill 15

Coordinates

Some problems on the GED Mathematics Tests will ask you to identify points on a graph. Points are identified by 2 numbers called **coordinates.** The coordinates represent an **ordered pair,** such as (2, −4). The first number is found on the horizontal axis, or the x-axis. This number is called the **x-coordinate.** The second number is called the **y-coordinate** and is found on the vertical axis, or y-axis. The **origin** is the point at the center of the graph with the coordinates (0, 0).

Locate points on a graph by starting at the origin and moving to the right or left along the x-axis and then up or down along the y-axis. For example, the point (3, −4) can be found by moving 3 units to the right from zero on the x-axis. Move to the right because the number 3 is positive. The negative sign in front of the 4 indicates to move 4 units down the y-axis from 3. The point (3, −4) corresponds to point F on the graph below.

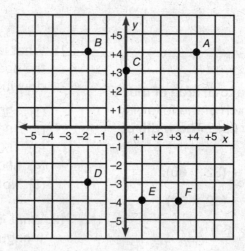

Use the sample coordinate graph above to answer the example question below.

EXAMPLE: The ordered pair (1, −4) corresponds to which point on the graph?

STEP 1 Start at the origin (0, 0).
Move 1 unit to the right on the x-axis.
Move right because the number is positive.

STEP 2 From the point in Step 1, move 4 units down on the y-axis.
Move down because the number is negative.

STEP 3 Choose the letter that is at this point.

ANSWER: point E

Practice the Skill

1. The coordinates of point *A* on the graph are (5, −3). What are the coordinates of point *B*?

   (1) (4, −2)
   (2) (−2, 4)
   (3) (−4, 2)
   (4) (−4, −2)
   (5) (−2, −4)

   HINT   Move left or right to find the *x*-coordinate, and move up and down to find the *y*-coordinate.

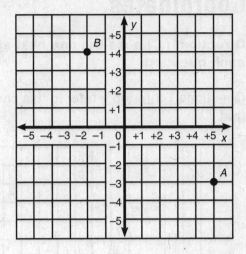

2. Which of the following ordered pairs will fall on the same vertical line as point *A* above?

   (1) (−2, −3)
   (2) (4, −3)
   (3) (−5, 3)
   (4) (−5, −3)
   (5) (5, 4)

   HINT   Which coordinate changes when you move left or right?

Answers and Solutions

1. (2) (−2, 4)
Step 1: Start at the origin (0, 0). Move 2 units to the left on the *x*-axis. The *x*-coordinate is −2 because it's two spaces left of the *y*-axis.

Step 2: From the point in Step 1, move 4 units up on *y*-axis. The *y*-coordinate is 4 because it's four spaces above the *x*-axis.

Step 3: Point *B* is at **(−2, 4)**.

2. (5) (5, 4)
Step 1: Write the ordered pair for point *A*.
                     (5, −3)

Step 2: The vertical lines cross the *x*-axis. They represent units on the *x*-axis. Look for the ordered pair answer choice that has the same *x*-coordinate as (5, −3).

Step 3: (5, 4) is the only answer choice that has 5 as the *x*-coordinate, the same as point *A*. Therefore, **(5, 4)** is on the same vertical line.

Coordinates

Directions: Choose the <u>one best answer</u> to each question.

<u>Questions 1 through 3</u> refer to this coordinate grid.

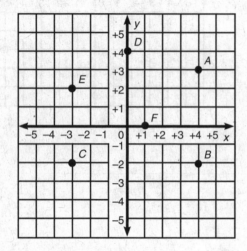

1. Point *B* on the graph refers to which of these ordered pairs?

    (1) (4, −2)
    (2) (−4, 2)
    (3) (4, 2)
    (4) (−2, 4)
    (5) (−2, −4)

2. The ordered pair (1, 0) corresponds to which point on the graph?

    (1) *A*
    (2) *C*
    (3) *D*
    (4) *E*
    (5) *F*

3. The ordered pair (−3, −2) corresponds to point *C* on the graph. Which point corresponds to (−3, 2)?

    (1) *A*
    (2) *C*
    (3) *D*
    (4) *E*
    (5) *F*

<u>Questions 4 through 7</u> refer to this coordinate grid.

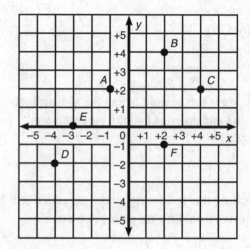

4. Point *E* refers to which ordered pair?

    (1) (3, 0)
    (2) (−3, 0)
    (3) (0, −3)
    (4) (0, 3)
    (5) Not enough information is given.

5. (−1, 2) corresponds to which point?

    (1) *A*
    (2) *B*
    (3) *C*
    (4) *E*
    (5) *F*

6. What is the first step to find point (2, 4)?

    (1) From (1, 1), move 2 units to the right.
    (2) From the origin, move 2 units to the left.
    (3) From the origin, move 2 units up.
    (4) From the origin, move 2 units to the right.
    (5) From the origin, move 4 units to the right.

7. Which two points have the same *x*-coordinate?

    (1) *A* and *C*
    (2) *B* and *C*
    (3) *B* and *F*
    (4) *D* and *F*
    (5) *F* and *A*

Questions 8 through 10 refer to this coordinate plane.

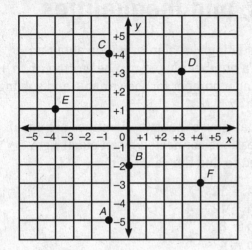

8. Point *A* is identified by which ordered pair?

   (1) (1, 5)
   (2) (−5, 0)
   (3) (−1, −5)
   (4) (−1, 0)
   (5) (−5, −1)

9. For which point is the *x*-value greater than the *y*-value?

   (1) *C*
   (2) *D*
   (3) *E*
   (4) *F*
   (5) Not enough information is given.

10. The ordered pair (−4, 1) corresponds to point *E* on the graph. Which point corresponds to (−1, 4)?

    (1) *A*
    (2) *B*
    (3) *C*
    (4) *D*
    (5) Not enough information is given.

11. Show the location of a point with the coordinates (−2, 5).

    Mark your answer on the coordinate plane grid below.

    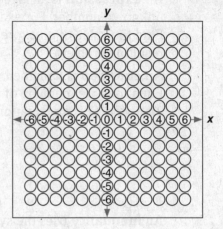

12. Show the location of a point represented by the ordered pair (3, 0).

    Mark your answer on the coordinate plane grid below.

    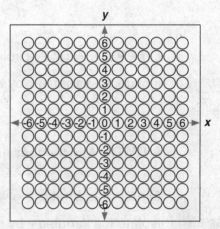

[TIP]

One way to remember that the *x*-coordinate is listed first in an ordered pair is that the letter *x* comes before *y* in the alphabet.

Answers and solutions start on page 120.

Algebra and Functions

Expressions, Equations, and Inequalities

An **expression** is an algebraic way of representing verbal information about an unknown number. For example, the phrase "a number plus 3" can be written as "$n + 3$." Find the value of an expression by substituting a number for the variable and solving the resulting problem.

An **equation** is a mathematical statement that shows that two quantities are equal. Equations are made up of two or more expressions connected by an equal sign. $2n + 4 = 12$ is an equation that can be solved to find the value of n.

$$2n + 4 = 12$$
$$2n + 4 - 4 = 12 - 4$$
$$2n = 8$$
$$n = 4$$

An **inequality** uses the symbols $>$ and $<$ to represent "greater than" and "less than." An inequality is solved the same way as an equation, with one exception: Multiplying or dividing both sides by a negative number changes the direction of the inequality symbol.

$$5 - n < 2$$
$$5 - 5 - n < 2 - 5 \qquad \text{Subtract 5 from each side.}$$
$$-n < -3 \qquad \text{Simplify.}$$
$$n > 3 \qquad \text{Multiply by } -1 \text{ and reverse the inequality sign.}$$

EXAMPLE 1: What is a solution to the inequality $n - 7 > 5$?

STEP 1 Isolate the variable x by adding 7 to both sides of the inequality.

$$n - 7 + 7 > 5 + 7$$
$$n > 12$$

ANSWER: Any number greater than 12 is a solution to the inequality.

EXAMPLE 2: What is the value of y that satisfies the equation $5y^2 + 11 = 31$?

STEP 1 Isolate the variable y by subtracting 11 from both sides of the equation.

$$5y^2 + 11 - 11 = 31 - 11$$
$$5y^2 = 20$$

STEP 2 Divide both sides by 5.

$$\frac{5y^2}{5} = \frac{20}{5}$$
$$y^2 = 4$$

STEP 3 Find the square root of each side.

$$\sqrt{y^2} = \sqrt{4}$$

ANSWER: $y = 2$

Practice the Skill

Try these examples. Choose the <u>one best answer</u> to each question. Then check your answers and the solutions.

1. Given the equation $2x - 5 = 4x + 3$, solve for x.

(1) 2
(2) 1
(3) −1
(4) −2
(5) −4

HINT Add or subtract first, and then complete the multiplication or division.

2. Which value below makes the inequality $4z^2 < 15$ true?

(1) −3
(2) −2
(3) 1
(4) 2
(5) 3

 Calculator Hint: To enter a negative number such as −3 on your calculator, key in:

$$3 \; \boxed{\pm}$$

Answers and Solutions

1. (5) −4

Step 1: Group the common terms on either side of the equation. Subtract $2x$ from both sides.

$$2x - 5 - 2x = 4x + 3 - 2x$$
$$-5 = 2x + 3$$

Step 2: Subtract 3 from both sides.

$$-5 - 3 = 2x + 3 - 3$$
$$-8 = 2x$$

Step 3: Divide both sides by 2.

$$\frac{-8}{2} = \frac{2x}{2}$$
$$-4 = x$$

2. (3) 1

Step 1: Substitute the answers into the inequality. Simplify by solving the squares.

$$4(-3)^2 < 15 = 4(9) < 15$$
$$4(-2)^2 < 15 = 4(4) < 15$$
$$4(1)^2 < 15 = 4(1) < 15$$
$$4(2)^2 < 15 = 4(4) < 15$$
$$4(3)^2 < 15 = 4(9) < 15$$

Step 2: Simplify. Then determine whether each inequality is true or false.

$$36 < 15$$
$$16 < 15$$
$$4 < 15$$
$$16 < 15$$
$$36 < 15$$

Step 3: The only true statement is $4 < 15$, so the only value that makes the inequality true is **1**.

Expressions, Equations, and Inequalities

Directions: Choose the <u>one best answer</u> to each question.

1. Evaluate $3x^2 - 4$ if $x = 5$.

   (1) 11
   (2) 63
   (3) 71
   (4) 121
   (5) 221

2. Which statement below represents the equation $2x - 3 = 7$?

   (1) three less than two times a number equals seven
   (2) seven equals twice three minus two
   (3) three more than two times a number equals seven
   (4) two times a number plus three equals seven
   (5) Not enough information is given.

Question 3 refers to this number line.

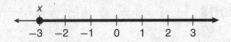

3. Which inequality is represented on the number line?

   (1) $x \leq -3$
   (2) $x > -3$
   (3) $x \geq -3$
   (4) $x \leq 3$
   (5) $x < -3$

4. If $x = 3$ and $y = 9$, what is the value of $\frac{x}{y}$?

   (1) 27
   (2) 12
   (3)   6
   (4)   3
   (5) $\frac{1}{3}$

5. For $p = 4(q - 7) + q$, find p if $q = 7$.

   (1)   7
   (2) 11
   (3) 25
   (4) 39
   (5) 63

6. Which of the following is the solution for $2a + 6 < 10$?

   (1) $a < -2$
   (2) $a < 2$
   (3) $a < 8$
   (4) $a > 2$
   (5) $a > 4$

7. Use the formula $A = lw$ to find w if $A = 34$ and $l = 8.5$.

   (1) $w =$ 4
   (2) $w =$ 24
   (3) $w =$ 40
   (4) $w = 108$
   (5) $w = 256$

8. Evaluate $7a - 3b$ if $a = 2$ and $b = -2$.

   (1)   4
   (2)   8
   (3) 15
   (4) 20
   (5) Not enough information is given.

9. What is the value of n if $\frac{n}{4} + 8 = 12$?

   Mark your answer in the circles in the grid below.

10. Given the formula $P = 2l + 2w$, what is P if $l = 16$ and $w = 12$?

(1) $P = 8$
(2) $P = 28$
(3) $P = 56$
(4) $P = 112$
(5) $P = 192$

11. Which equation represents the phrase "eight more than the square of four is the same as three less than six"?

(1) $8 - 4^2 = 6 - 3$
(2) $4^2(8) = 6 - 3$
(3) $4^2 + 8 = 6 - 3$
(4) $4^2 + 8 = 3 - 6$
(5) $4^2 - 8 = 6 - 3$

12. For which value of z below is the inequality $6z < -3$ true?

(1) -1
(2) 0
(3) 1
(4) 2
(5) 3

13. Evaluate $3r^2 - 4s$, if $r = 7$ and $s = -3$.

(1) 429
(2) 159
(3) 135
(4) 86
(5) Not enough information is given.

14. Given the formula $C = \pi d$, what is d if $C = 66$ and $\pi = \frac{22}{7}$? Round your answer to the nearest integer.

(1) $d = 4$
(2) $d = 21$
(3) $d = 77$
(4) $d = 198$
(5) $d = 207$

15. Which graph is the solution to the inequality, $3x < 6$?

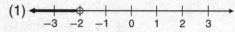

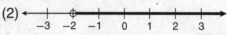

16. Given the equation $y = 5x(z + 7)$, what is y if $z = -4$ and $x = 2$?

Mark your answer in the circles in the grid below.

/	/	/	
.	.	.	.
0	0	0	0	0
1	1	1	1	1
2	2	2	2	2
3	3	3	3	3
4	4	4	4	4
5	5	5	5	5
6	6	6	6	6
7	7	7	7	7
8	8	8	8	8
9	9	9	9	9

[**TIP**]

To check an inequality or the solution to an equation, substitute the answer into the original problem and solve.

Answers and solutions start on page 121.

KEY Skill 17

Algebra and Functions

Linear Equations

An equation with both *x* and *y* variables and no exponents is called a **linear equation.** When graphed, a linear equation will form a straight line as shown on the graph below.

Graph a line by finding two points and drawing a straight line through them. Begin by choosing a value for *x* and solving the equation for *y*. Then repeat the process with a different *x*-value. Graph both points and then draw a line through them. The linear equation of the line on the graph below is $y = (x \div 2) - 1$. Verify the equation by substituting the known coordinates (2, 0) and then (−4, −3).

$$0 = (2 \div 2) - 1 \qquad\qquad -3 = (-4 \div 2) - 1$$
$$0 = 0 \qquad\qquad\qquad -3 = -3$$

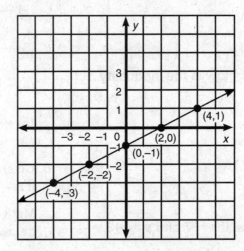

The **slope** of a line is a measure of its steepness. Slope is represented by the letter *m* and is commonly referred to as *rise/run*. Find the slope of a line by choosing two points on the line and dividing the difference in *y*-values by the difference in *x*-values.

Slope $= \dfrac{y_2 - y_1}{x_2 - x_1}$, where (x_1, y_1) and (x_2, y_2) are two points on the line.

The equation $y = mx + b$ represents the **slope-intercept form** for the equation of a line. In this equation, *m* represents slope and *b* represents the *y*-intercept. The *y*-intercept is the *y*-coordinate of the point where the line crosses the *y*-axis in the form (0, *b*). The *x*-coordinate will always be 0.

....

EXAMPLE: What is the *y*-intercept of the line represented by $y = -2x + 5$?

STEP 1 Write the slope-intercept form for the equation of a line.

$$y = mx + b \longrightarrow y = -2x + 5$$

STEP 2 Find the value of *b*, and write the ordered pair form for a *y*-intercept.

$$b = 5, \text{ so the ordered pair is } (0, 5).$$

ANSWER: The y-intercept is (0, 5).

....

74 *Keys to GED® Success: Mathematics*

Practice the Skill

Try these examples. Choose the one best answer to each question. Then check your answers and the solutions.

1. Show the location of the y-intercept of the line with the equation $y = 3x - 1$. Mark your answer on the coordinate plane grid below.

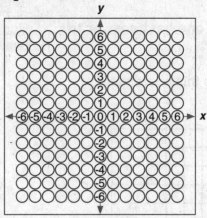

HINT To check your answer, input two other x-values into the equation and graph the line.

2. What is the equation for a line that has a slope of $\frac{2}{3}$ and contains the point (0, 6)?

(1) $y = \frac{-2}{3}x$

(2) $y = \frac{-2}{3}x + 6$

(3) $y = \frac{2}{3}x - 6$

(4) $y = \frac{2}{3}x + 6$

(5) $y = 6x + \frac{2}{3}$

Calculator Hint: Insert any fraction in the form of $\frac{1}{x}$, such as $\frac{1}{5}$, by keying in:

1 $\boxed{a^b/c}$ 5

[Answers and Solutions]

1.

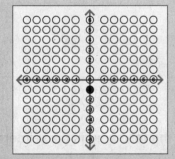

Step 1: Write the slope-intercept form of an equation for a line.
$$y = mx + b \longrightarrow y = 3x - 1$$

Step 2: Find the value for b: −1. Write the ordered pair for the y-intercept.
$$(0, b) = (0, -1)$$

Step 3: Plot **(0, −1)** on the coordinate grid.

2. (4) $y = \frac{2}{3}x + 6$

Step 1: Write the slope-intercept form for the equation of a line.
$$y = mx + b$$

Step 2: In the equation, the slope is $m = \frac{2}{3}$.

Step 3: The coordinate (0, 6) is the y-intercept, b, because it has an x-coordinate of 0, so b = 6.

Step 4: Substitute the known values for b and m into the slope-intercept equation.

$$y = \frac{2}{3}x + 6$$

Linear Equations

Directions: Choose the <u>one best answer</u> to each question.

<u>Questions 1 and 2</u> refer to this coordinate plane.

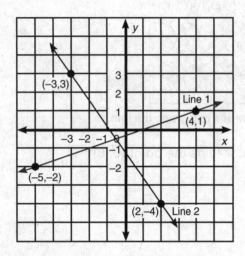

1. Which expression represents the slope of Line 2?

   (1) $\dfrac{-3-3}{2+4}$

   (2) $\dfrac{-4-3}{2-(-3)}$

   (3) $\dfrac{2-(-3)}{3-(-3)}$

   (4) $\dfrac{-4}{3}$

   (5) $\dfrac{2-3}{-4+3}$

2. What is the slope of Line 1 on the graph above?

   (1) $\dfrac{5}{7}$

   (2) 3

   (3) $\dfrac{1}{3}$

   (4) −1

   (5) $\dfrac{9}{2}$

<u>Questions 3 through 5</u> refer to this coordinate plane.

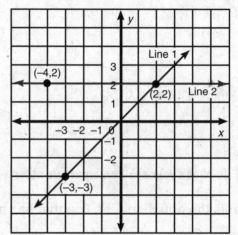

3. Which of the following expressions represents the slope of Line 1?

   (1) $\dfrac{2-3}{2+3}$

   (2) $\dfrac{-2+3}{-3+2}$

   (3) $\dfrac{2-(-3)}{2-(-3)}$

   (4) $\dfrac{-3}{2}$

   (5) $\dfrac{2}{-3}$

4. Which of the following numbers is the slope of a line that would be parallel to Line 2?

   (1) −2

   (2) 0

   (3) 1

   (4) 2

   (5) 6

5. Which of the following is the *y*-intercept for Line 2?

   (1) (2, 2)

   (2) (2, 0)

   (3) (0, 2)

   (4) (0, 0)

   (5) (−4, 0)

6. If a line is drawn through the points (4, 1) and (2, −4), what will the slope of the line be?

(1) −5

(2) −2

(3) $-\dfrac{5}{2}$

(4) $\dfrac{5}{2}$

(5) $\dfrac{2}{5}$

Questions 7 and 8 refer to this coordinate plane.

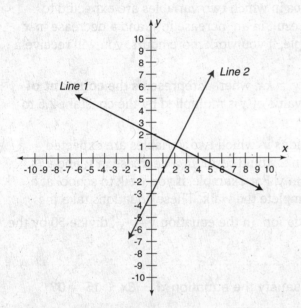

7. What are the coordinates of the point that is contained in both lines on the graph above?

(1) (0, −3)

(2) (0, 2)

(3) (1, 2)

(4) (2, 1)

(5) (4, 0)

8. What is the linear equation for Line 2 on the graph?

(1) $y = -3x + 2$

(2) $y = -2x + 3$

(3) $y = \dfrac{1}{2}x + 2$

(4) $y = x + 2$

(5) $y = 2x - 3$

9. The line on a graph passes through the origin (0, 0) and the point (5, 3). What is the slope of the line?

(1) 5

(2) 3

(3) $\dfrac{5}{3}$

(4) $\dfrac{3}{5}$

(5) 0

10. Parallel lines have the same slope but different y-intercepts. Which of the following lines is parallel to the line $y = \dfrac{-1}{2}x - 1$?

(1) $y = 2x + 1$

(2) $y = \dfrac{-1}{-2}x - 1$

(3) $y = \dfrac{-1}{2}x + 1$

(4) $y = \dfrac{1}{2}x - 1$

(5) $y = 2x - 1$

11. Show the location of the y-intercept of the line with the equation $4x + y = -2$.

Mark your answer on the coordinate plane grid below.

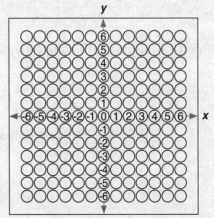

Answers and solutions start on page 122.

Functions

A **function** is a mathematical equation that describes the relationship between two variables. Linear equations are one type of function.

Quadratic equations are functions that contain at least one x^2 term. Solve quadratic equations by factoring or by substituting values into the equation. An example of a quadratic equation is $x^2 + 5x + 6 = 0$.

Exponential equations are functions that have a constant raised to a variable power, such as $y = x^2$. A **constant** is a number that does not change. Solve problems involving exponential functions by substituting values into the equation.

Direct variation equations are functions in which two variables are expected to change together. An increase in x would result in an increase in y, and a decrease in x would result in a decrease in y. For example, if you work more hours, you will receive a larger paycheck.

Direct variation equations have the form $y = kx$, where k represents the **constant of variation.** In the equation $y = 2.5x$, the value of x is multiplied by the constant 2.5 to find the value of y.

Indirect variation equations are functions in which two variables are expected to change in opposite ways. An increase in x would result in a decrease in y, and a decrease in x would result in an increase in y. For example, if you walk to school at a faster rate, it will take you less time to complete the walk. These equations take the form $y = \frac{k}{x}$, where k is the constant of variation. In the equation $y = \frac{50}{x}$, divide 50 by the value of x to find the value of y.

....

EXAMPLE: What are the values of x that satisfy the equation $x^2 - 8x + 15 = 0$?

STEP 1 Factor the quadratic expression.

$$x^2 - 8x + 15 = 0$$
$$(x - 5)(x - 3) = 0$$

STEP 2 For each factor, determine the value of x that will make that factor equal to 0.

If $x - 5 = 0$, then $x = 5$.
If $x - 3 = 0$, then $x = 3$.

STEP 3 Check both values by substituting them into the original equation. Then solve.

$$5^2 - 8(5) + 15 = 0 \qquad\qquad 3^2 - 8(3) + 15 = 0$$
$$25 - 40 + 15 = 0 \qquad\qquad 9 - 24 + 15 = 0$$

ANSWER: The two values are 5 and 3.

....

Practice the Skill

Try these examples. Choose the <u>one best answer</u> to each question. Then check your answers and the solutions.

1. Joshua works at the local coffee shop. He earns a weekly salary of $450 plus a bonus of $0.25 for every cup of coffee he sells. If Joshua earned a total of $534 last week, in which of the following equations does c represent the number of cups of coffee he sold in the week?

   (1) $450 + 0.25c = 534$
   (2) $0.25c + 450 + 0.25 = 534$
   (3) $c + 450 = 534$
   (4) $0.25c \div 450 = 534$
   (5) $0.25c \times 450 = 534$

HINT Try writing the equation in words first, and then substitute the given values from the question.

2. Which of the following pairs satisfies the equation $x^2 + 4x - 12 = 0$?

   (1) −6 and 2
   (2) −2 and −4
   (3) −2 and 6
   (4) 2 and −2
   (5) 4 and −12

 Calculator Hint: The Casio fx-260*SOLAR* calculator will perform operations in the correct order when you enter the numbers in the problem from left to right.

Answers and Solutions

1. (1) $450 + 0.25c = 534$
Step 1: In words, write an equation that represents the information given:

Joshua's weekly salary plus a bonus based on the number of coffees he sells equals the total amount of money he made last week.

Step 2: Match terms from the question to each part of the word equation from Step 1.

450 = Joshua's weekly salary
$0.25c$ = the amount of Joshua's bonus per coffee sold, multiplied by the unknown number of coffees sold
534 = total money Joshua made last week

Step 3: Substitute the terms into the word equation from Step 1.

$$450 + 0.25c = 534$$

2. (1) −6 and 2
Step 1: Substitute one potential solution from each answer choice into the equation.

(1) $x = 2$; $2^2 + 4(2) - 12 = 0 = 0$
(2) $x = -4$; $(-4)^2 + 4(-4) - 12 = -12 \neq 0$
(3) $x = 6$; $6^2 + 4(6) - 12 = 48 \neq 0$
(4) $x = -2$; $(-2)^2 + 4(-2) - 12 = -16 \neq 0$
(5) $x = -12$; $(-12)^2 + 4(-12) - 12 = 84 \neq 0$

Step 2: Option 1 is the only pair that has a solution that satisfies the equation. Check the other solution in option 1.

$$x = -6; (-6)^2 + 4(-6) - 12 = 0 = 0$$

The solutions are $x = -6$ and $x = 2$.

Functions

Directions: Choose the <u>one best answer</u> to each question.

<u>Question 1</u> refers to this table.

x	−4	−2	0	2	4
y	−19	−11	−3		13

1. The function $y = 4x - 3$ has been used to create the table above. What number is missing from the table?

   (1) −5
   (2) −2
   (3)   5
   (4)   8
   (5) Not enough information is given.

2. If y varies indirectly as x, and $y = 24$ when $x = 48$, what is the constant of variation, k?

   (1)   0.5
   (2)   2
   (3)   12
   (4)   72
   (5) 1152

3. In Spring Forest, the total cost of a purchase including tax, c, can be found using the direct variation equation $c = 1.08p$, where p is the price of the item before tax. If Susan bought a DVD for $19.98, including tax, what was the price of the DVD before tax?

   (1) $18.50
   (2) $18.90
   (3) $19.00
   (4) $21.06
   (5) $21.58

4. A certain type of bacteria is found to multiply exponentially according to the formula $p = 10^t$, where p is the population after t hours. What will the population of the bacteria be after 5 hours?

   (1)   1,000
   (2)   5,000
   (3)   10,000
   (4)   100,000
   (5)   1,000,000

5. The Raleigh High Pep Club is planning to deliver 200 coats to a shelter. The more volunteers they recruit, the fewer deliveries each volunteer will have to make. Which type of function best models this situation?

   (1) linear
   (2) quadratic
   (3) exponential
   (4) direct variation
   (5) indirect variation

6. For the function $y = \frac{x}{6}$, which of the following values for x results in a fractional value of y (that is, y is not a whole number)?

   (1) 18
   (2) 36
   (3) 48
   (4) 64
   (5) 66

7. Use the equation $y = 3^x$ to find the value of y when $x = 4$.

   (1)   9
   (2)   12
   (3)   27
   (4)   81
   (5)   243

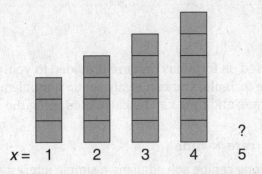

x = 1   2   3   4   5

8. Which function describes the figure above?

    (1) $y = 2x + 1$
    (2) $y = x + 1$
    (3) $y = x + 2$
    (4) $y = x - 2$
    (5) $y = 2x - 2$

9. If the pattern continues, how many blocks will there be when $x = 5$?

    (1)   5
    (2)   7
    (3)   8
    (4)   9
    (5) 11

10. Tina is selling t-shirts at a football game for $12 each. Which equation could be used to find the total amount of money she will earn, a, if she sells n t-shirts?

    (1) $a = 12 + n$
    (2) $a = \frac{12}{n}$
    (3) $a = 12n$
    (4) $n = 12a$
    (5) Not enough information is given.

[TIP]

When trying to find the solutions for a quadratic equation on the GED Mathematics Tests, you do not need to factor the equation first. Working backward and substituting the answer choices into the equation is an easier, faster way to solve. Use this strategy to save valuable test time.

Question 11 refers to this table.

x	−4	1	4		11
y	−5	5	11		25

11. The function $y = 2x + 3$ has been used to create the table above. What number is missing from the y-row in the table?

    (1) −1
    (2)   7
    (3) 14
    (4) 23
    (5) Not enough information is given.

 12. The "rule of 72" is an indirect variation equation that determines how long it takes an investment to double in value. The equation is $t = \frac{72}{r}$, where t is the number of years it takes an investment to double and r is the interest rate as a percent. How many years will it take an investment of $5,000 to double at an interest rate of 6%?

Mark your answer in the circles in the grid below.

Answers and solutions start on page 123.

Skill 19

Algebraic Formulas

Some questions on the GED Test will be based on formulas that are provided to you. By substituting the correct numbers into the formula, you can easily set up a problem and solve it. Problems involving distance, rate, and time can be calculated using the distance formula below.

distance = rate × time

Problems involving simple interest calculations can be solved using a simple interest formula. Remember that in this formula the principal is the initial amount of money, the rate is the percent of interest in decimal form, and the time is the length of time in years.

interest = principal × rate × time

Problems involving the total cost of a number of items can be solved with the total cost formula below.

total cost = number of units × price per unit

To use any of the formulas described above, substitute the values you know into the formula and use algebra to solve for the unknown value.

EXAMPLE 1: If roofing shingles sell for $17.49 per square, what expression will give the cost for 10 squares?

STEP 1 Choose the total cost formula.

total cost = number of units × price per unit

STEP 2 Substitute the known values into the formula.

total cost = 10 squares × $17.49

ANSWER: total cost = $17.49(10)

EXAMPLE 2: Joe put $500 into his savings account. After 3 years, he received a total of $150 in interest. What is the annual interest rate?

STEP 1 Choose the simple interest rate formula

interest = principal × rate × time

STEP 2 To solve for the rate, divide by the principal multiplied by time.

$$\frac{\text{interest}}{\text{principal} \times \text{time}} = \text{rate}$$

STEP 3 Substitute the known values into the formula.

$$\text{rate} = \frac{150}{500 \times 3} = \frac{150}{1500} = 0.1$$

STEP 4 Convert the decimal to a percent by multiplying by 100 and adding a percent sign.

$$0.1 \times 100 = 10\%$$

ANSWER: 10% rate

Practice the Skill

Try these examples. Choose the one best answer to each question. Then check your answers and the solutions.

1. A shipment of jeans cost $957.60. The jeans will be marked up by 30%. What is the expression for how many pairs of jeans are in the shipment?

   (1) $957.60 × 0.30
   (2) $957.60 ÷ 0.30
   (3) $957.60 − 0.30 + 400
   (4) $957.60 × 400
   (5) Not enough information is given.

HINT Choose the formula that matches the information given, and then substitute the known values.

2. If you travel an average of 50 miles per hour on a trip that takes 3 hours 15 minutes to complete, how many miles did you travel?

   (1) 165
   (2) 162.5
   (3) 157.5
   (4) 152.5
   (5) 150

Calculator Hint: To convert 15 minutes to a decimal part of an hour, use your calculator to divide 15 by 60. The screen will display 0.25.

Answers and Solutions

1. (5) Not enough information is given.

Step 1: Choose the total cost formula.

total cost = number of jeans × price per jeans

Step 2: Solve for number of units (jeans).

$$\frac{\text{total cost}}{\text{price per jeans}} = \text{number of jeans}$$

Step 3: Substitute for the known values.

$$\frac{957.60}{\text{price per jeans}} = \text{number of jeans}$$

Step 4: There is **not enough information given.** You need to know the price per pair of jeans to solve the formula for the total number of pairs of jeans.

2. (2) 162.5

Step 1: Choose the distance formula.

distance = rate × time

Step 2: Substitute in the known values.

distance = 50 mph × 3 hours 15 minutes

Step 3: Convert the time into a decimal.

3 hours 15 minutes = $3\frac{15}{60}$ = $3\frac{1}{4}$ = 3.25 hours

Step 4: Solve for distance.

50 mph × 3.25 hours = **162.5** miles

Algebraic Formulas

Directions: Choose the <u>one best answer</u> to each question.

1. A jet travels at an average speed of 200 miles per hour. At this rate, how many hours will it take the jet to travel 1,000 miles?

   (1) 200
   (2) 100
   (3) 50
   (4) 5
   (5) 1

 2. Sue borrowed $300 at an annual interest rate of 14.5%. Which expression shows the amount of interest she will pay if she pays the loan back in 1 year?

   (1) 300(14.5)
   (2) 300 ÷ 0.145
   (3) 300 + 14.5
   (4) 300(1.45)
   (5) 300(0.145)

<u>Question 3</u> refers to this table.

Shipment Number	Shipment Cost	Per Unit Cost
1	$ 9,500	$1,600
2	$11,500	$1,420
3	$12,000	$1,500

3. The table above shows the cost of three shipments of computers and price paid per computer. How many computers were in shipment number 3?

   (1) 15
   (2) 12
   (3) 8
   (4) 6
   (5) 3

 4. A case of 24 cans of juice costs $7.20. Linda bought 3 cases. Which expression represents the amount she paid per can?

   (1) $7.20(24) ÷ 3
   (2) $7.20 + 3(24)
   (3) $7.20 − 24
   (4) 24 ÷ $7.20
   (5) $7.20 ÷ 24

5. How many years will it take to make $625 in interest if $5000 is deposited into a savings account that pays 6.25% annual interest?

   (1) 5
   (2) 2
   (3) 1.28
   (4) 1
   (5) 0.02

6. A bullet train can travel very fast. If a bullet train travels 150 miles in 90 minutes, what is the speed of the train in miles per hour?

   Mark your answer in the circles in the grid below.

Question 7 refers to this table.

John's Running Log

Distance	Rate	Time
4 miles	7.5 mph	32 minutes
5 miles		41 minutes
6 miles	5.8 mph	1 hour 2 minutes

7. John went running three times last week. He recorded the distance he ran and the time it took him to complete each run in the table above. He began to calculate the rate of his run in miles per hour. What is the rate (in mph) for his 5-mile run?

(1) 0.12
(2) 7.2
(3) 7.4
(4) 8.8
(5) Not enough information is given.

8. One brand of roof sealer costs $12.99 for a 5-gallon can. What is the approximate cost per gallon?

(1) less than $1
(2) between $1 and $2
(3) between $2 and $3
(4) between $4 and $5
(5) more than $5

 9. Linda took out a loan to pay for a new car. Her bank charges $8\frac{1}{2}\%$ annual interest for a new car loan to be paid back in 5 years. If Linda will pay $5,100 in interest, how much did Linda borrow?

(1) $21,675
(2) $12,000
(3) $11,164
(4) $ 8,500
(5) $ 165

10. A three-pound bag of onions costs $1.29. Which expression could be used to find the cost of one onion if there are 10 onions in the bag?

(1) $1.29 ÷ 3
(2) $1.29 × 3
(3) $1.29 ÷ 10
(4) $1.29 + 3(10)
(5) 10 ÷ $1.29

11. George is practicing for a canoe race across a lake. The lake is 1 mile wide. George has been told that if he can average a rate of 4 miles per hour that he has a good chance to win the race. George calculates that it will take him 15 minutes to cross the lake. What formula did George use to calculate his time?

(1) complex interest formula
(2) distance formula
(3) simple interest formula
(4) total cost formula
(5) Not enough information is given.

 12. If a pound of curry powder is 16 ounces and costs $12, how much does one ounce cost?

Mark your answer in the circles in the grid below.

/	/	/	
.	.	.	.	.
0	0	0	0	0
1	1	1	1	1
2	2	2	2	2
3	3	3	3	3
4	4	4	4	4
5	5	5	5	5
6	6	6	6	6
7	7	7	7	7
8	8	8	8	8
9	9	9	9	9

TIP

Be sure that all numbers are in the correct form and in the correct units before substituting them into a formula.

Answers and solutions start on page 124.

Skill 20

Algebra Word Problems

Many of the word problems found on the GED Mathematics Tests involve **algebraic expressions** and **equations.** Some of these problems ask you to set up the solution. Others ask you to find the solution. Begin to solve **algebra word problems** by choosing a variable to represent one quantity in the problem. Then create other expressions to represent other important quantities. Write an equation in words, and then substitute the expressions for the words to create an algebraic expression.

EXAMPLE 1: Rico has $6 more than Vanessa. If the total amount of money they have is $23, write an equation that could be used to find the amount each person has.

STEP 1 Assign variables and write expressions for each quantity.

x = amount Vanessa has $x + 6$ = amount Rico has $23 = total amount

STEP 2 Use your variables and expressions to form an equation.

$$x + (x + 6) = 23$$

ANSWER: $x + (x + 6) = 23$

EXAMPLE 2: James has 5 more quarters than dimes. He has 13 coins in all. If x represents the number of dimes, which equation could be used to find the number of dimes and quarters James has?

STEP 1 Assign variables and write expressions for each quantity.

x = number of dimes $x + 5$ = number of quarters   13 = total number of coins

STEP 2 Set up an equation in words to represent the problem

total number of coins = number of dimes + number of quarters

STEP 3 Substitute the expressions from Step 1 into the equation in Step 2, and then solve.

$$13 = x + x + 5$$
$$13 = 2x + 5 \qquad \text{group like terms}$$
$$13 - 5 = 2x + 5 - 5 \qquad \text{subtract 5 from each side}$$
$$8 = 2x$$
$$8 \div 2 = 2x \div 2 \qquad \text{divide by 2}$$
$$x = 4 \qquad \text{solve}$$

STEP 4 Substitute the value of x into the expression for the number of dimes and quarters.

$x = 4$ = number of dimes $x + 5 = 4 + 5 = 9$ = number of quarters

ANSWER: 4 dimes and 9 quarters

Practice the Skill

1. Together Rene and Carleta have $15. Rene has $3 more than Carleta. How much money does Rene have?

   (1) $ 1
   (2) $ 3
   (3) $ 6
   (4) $ 9
   (5) $12

    HINT What expression represents the amount of money Rene has?

2. The plans for a rectangular dog kennel give the dimensions as $2x$ feet by x feet. Solve for the area if $x = 4$.

   (1) 8 ft²
   (2) 18 ft²
   (3) 24 ft²
   (4) 32 ft²
   (5) 64 ft²

   Calculator Hint: To find the square of a number on your calculator, such as 4^2, key in:

   $$4 \boxed{x^2}$$

Answers and Solutions

1. (4) $9
Step 1: Choose a variable to represent one quantity, and then write an expression to represent the other quantity.

  Carleta's money = y
  Rene's money = $y + 3$

Step 2: Set up an equation in words to represent the problem.
  Carleta's money + Rene's money = $15

Step 3: Substitute the expressions from Step 1 into the equation in Step 2, and then solve.

  $y + y + 3 = 15$
   $2y + 3 = 15$ group like terms
  $2y + 3 - 3 = 15 - 3$ subtract 3
     $2y = 12$ divide by 2
      $y = 6$ solve

Step 4: Substitute the value of y into the expression for Carleta's money and Rene's money.

      $y = 6$ = Carleta's money
  $y + 3 = 6 + 3 = \$9$ = Rene's money

2. (4) 32 ft²
Step 1: Choose a variable to represent one quantity, and then write an expression to represent the other quantity.

    dimension 1 = x
    dimension 2 = $2x$

Step 2: Set up an equation in words to represent the problem.
  dimension 1 × dimension 2 = kennel area

Step 3: Substitute the expressions from Step 1 into the equation in Step 2.
  $x \times 2x$ = kennel area
    $2x^2$ = kennel area group like terms

Step 4: Substitute the value of x into the expression for the kennel area and solve.
     $2x^2$ = kennel area
    $2(4)^2$ = kennel area
    $2(16)$ = kennel area
    32 ft² = kennel area

Algebra Word Problems

Directions: Choose the <u>one best answer</u> to each question.

1. Hector earns three times as much today as he did on his first job 5 years ago. If he makes $75,000 per year now, which expression can be used to find how much he made on his first job?

   (1) $\frac{n}{3}$
   (2) $n - 3$
   (3) $3n$
   (4) $3(n - 3)$
   (5) $n + 3$

 2. The Alexanders bought 9 movie tickets for a total cost of $90.00. Each child's ticket cost $6, and each adult's ticket cost $12. How many children's tickets did the Alexanders buy?

   (1) 6
   (2) 5
   (3) 4
   (4) 3
   (5) Not enough information is given.

Questions 3 refers to this figure.

$$4x$$

3. The area of a rectangular garden is 64 square meters. What are the dimensions of the garden?

   (1) 2 m × 8 m
   (2) 3 m × 12 m
   (3) 4 m × 16 m
   (4) 5 m × 20 m
   (5) 6 m × 36 m

4. Alfredo is 5 years older than John, and Maria is 4 years younger than John. If the sum of their ages is 34, which equation can be used to find John's age?

   (1) $x + 5 + x - 4 = 34$
   (2) $x + x + 5 + x - 4 = 34$
   (3) $5x + 4x = 34$
   (4) $x + 1 = 34$
   (5) $3x = 34$

 5. A car rental agency charged Robert $29 per day plus $0.60 per mile for each mile over 100 miles to rent a car. How much will Robert pay if he keeps the car for 5 days and travels 156 miles?

   (1) $283.60
   (2) $178.60
   (3) $145.00
   (4) $ 93.60
   (5) $ 83.60

6. Last week pet owners attended a pet show. If twice as many cat owners as dog owners attended the show, how many cat owners attended?

   (1) 3
   (2) 6
   (3) 9
   (4) 16
   (5) Not enough information is given.

> **TIP**
>
> For problems involving area or perimeter of geometric figures, make a sketch of the figure and label the parts. This will help you keep track of all the measurements.

7. A nursery worker earns x dollars for working 25 hours. Which expression could be used to find how much the worker would earn if he worked 30 hours?

(1) $30x$

(2) $\frac{30}{25}x$

(3) $\frac{25}{30}x$

(4) $25x$

(5) $5x$

8. At 9 A.M., the temperature was $-5°C$. By 9 P.M., the temperature had dropped x degrees. Which expression represents the temperature reading at 9 P.M.?

(1) $5 - x$
(2) $-5 - x$
(3) $-5 + x$
(4) $5x$
(5) -5

9. Two numbers have a sum of 18. One number is 4 more than the other. What is the value of the larger number?

Mark your answer in the circles in the grid below.

10. Together, two teachers have a total of 40 students. Ms. Felder has 6 more students than Mr. Pearce. How many students does Ms. Felder have?

(1) 6
(2) 17
(3) 23
(4) 27
(5) 34

11. Monica has a $1.50 off coupon and a $3.00 mail-in rebate certificate for a clock. Which expression shows how much she will pay for the clock after the rebate and the coupon if p represents the price of the clock?

(1) $p - \$1.50 + \$3.00$
(2) $p + \$1.50 - \$3.00$
(3) $p + \$1.50 + \$3.00$
(4) $p - \$1.50 - \$3.00$
(5) Not enough information is given.

Question 12 refers to this figure.

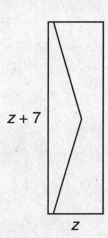

$z + 7$

z

12. Which of the following equations can be used to find the width of the envelope if the perimeter is 54 inches?

(1) $2(z + 7) = 54$
(2) $7z^2 = 54$
(3) $z + 7 = 54$
(4) $2z + 2(z + 7) = 54$
(5) $z + 7z = 54$

Answers and solutions start on page 125.

Test Form PA
Mathematics Part I

Tests of
General Educational
Development

Mathematics
Official GED Practice Test
Calculator Use Allowed

GED Testing Service
American Council on Education

MATHEMATICS

Tests of General Educational Development

Directions

The Mathematics Test consists of questions intended to measure general mathematics skills and problem-solving ability. The questions are based on short readings that often include a graph, chart, or figure.

You will have 23 minutes to complete the 13 questions in this booklet. Work carefully, but do not spend too much time on any one question. Be sure you answer every question.

Formulas you may need are given on page 4. Only some of the questions will require you to use a formula. Not all the formulas given will be needed.

Some questions contain more information than you will need to solve the problem; other questions do not give enough information. If the question does not give enough information to solve the problem, the correct answer choice is "Not enough information is given."

The use of calculators is allowed.

Do not write in this test booklet. The test administrator will give you blank paper for your calculations. Record your answers on the separate answer sheet provided. Be sure all information is properly recorded on the answer sheet.

To record your answers, fill in the numbered circle on the answer sheet that corresponds to the answer you select for each question in the test booklet.

FOR EXAMPLE:

If a grocery bill totaling $15.75 is paid with a $20.00 bill, how much change should be returned?

(1) $5.25
(2) $4.75
(3) $4.25
(4) $3.75
(5) $3.25

(On Answer Sheet)

① ② ● ④ ⑤

The correct answer is "$4.25"; therefore, answer space 3 would be marked on the answer sheet.

Do not rest the point of your pencil on the answer sheet while you are considering your answer. Make no stray or unnecessary marks. If you change an answer, erase your first mark completely. Mark only one answer space for each question; multiple answers will be scored as incorrect. Do not fold or crease your answer sheet. All test materials must be returned to the test administrator.

GO ON TO THE NEXT PAGE

Mathematics

Mixed numbers, such as $3\frac{1}{2}$, cannot be entered in the alternate format grid. Instead, represent them as decimal numbers (in this case, 3.5) or fractions (in this case, 7/2). No answer can be a negative number, such as -8.

To record your answer for an alternate format question
- begin in any column that will allow your answer to be entered;
- write your answer in the boxes on the top row;
- in the column beneath a fraction bar or decimal point (if any) and each number in your answer, fill in the bubble representing that character;
- leave blank any unused column.

EXAMPLE:

The scale on a map indicates that 1/2 inch represents an actual distance of 120 miles. In inches, how far apart on the map will two towns be if the actual distance between them is 180 miles?

The answer to the above example is 3/4, or 0.75, inches. A few examples of how the answer could be gridded are shown below.

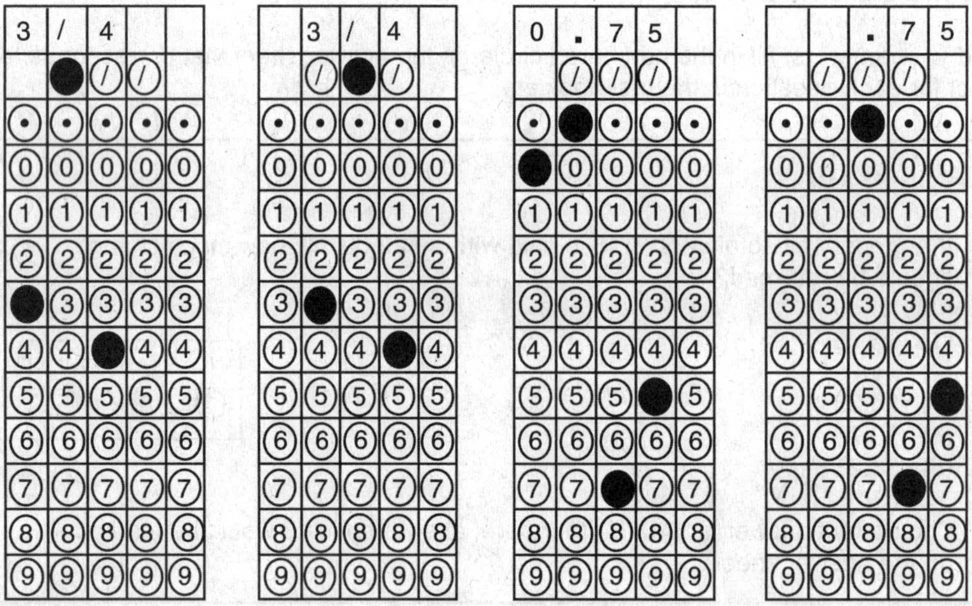

Points to remember:

- The answer sheet will be machine scored. **The circles must be filled in correctly.**
- Mark no more than one circle in any column.
- Grid only one answer even if there is more than one correct answer.
- Mixed numbers such as $3\frac{1}{2}$ must be gridded as 3.5 or 7/2.

GO ON TO THE NEXT PAGE

CALCULATOR DIRECTIONS

To prepare the calculator for use the ***first*** time, press the [ON] (upper-rightmost) key. "DEG" will appear at the top-center of the screen and "0." at the right. This indicates the calculator is in the proper format for all your calculations.

To prepare the calculator for ***another*** question, press the [ON] or the red [AC] key. This clears any entries made previously.

To do any arithmetic, enter the expression as it is written. Press [=] (equals sign) when finished.

EXAMPLE A: $8 - 3 + 9$

First press [ON] or [AC].
Enter the following:

[8] [–] [3] [+] [9] [=]

The correct answer is 14.

If an expression in parentheses is to be multiplied by a number, press [x] (multiplication sign) between the number and the parenthesis sign.

EXAMPLE B: $6(8 + 5)$

First press [ON] or [AC].
Enter the following:

[6] [x] [( ] [8] [+] [5] [ )] [=]

The correct answer is 78.

To find the square root of a number
- enter the number;
- press the [SHIFT] (upper-leftmost) key ("SHIFT" appears at top-left of the screen);
- press [x^2] (third from the left on top row) to access its second function: square root.

DO NOT press [SHIFT] and [x^2] at the same time.

EXAMPLE C: $\sqrt{64}$

First press [ON] or [AC].
Enter the following:

[6] [4] [SHIFT] [x^2] [=]

The correct answer is 8.

To enter a negative number such as -8
- enter the number without the negative sign (enter 8);
- press the "change sign" ([+/-]) key which is directly above the [7] key.

All arithmetic can be done with positive and/or negative numbers.

EXAMPLE D: $-8 - -5$

First press [ON] or [AC].
Enter the following:

[8] [+/-] [–] [5] [+/-] [=]

The correct answer is -3.

DO NOT BEGIN TAKING THIS TEST UNTIL TOLD TO DO SO

Component: 9993949159
Kit: **ISBN 0-7398-5433-X**

FORMULAS

AREA of a:

square	Area = side^2
rectangle	Area = length × width
parallelogram	Area = base × height
triangle	Area = $\frac{1}{2}$ × base × height
trapezoid	Area = $\frac{1}{2}$ × (base$_1$ + base$_2$) × height
circle	Area = π × radius^2; π is approximately equal to 3.14.

PERIMETER of a:

square	Perimeter = 4 × side
rectangle	Perimeter = 2 × length + 2 × width
triangle	Perimeter = side$_1$ + side$_2$ + side$_3$

CIRCUMFERENCE of a circle

Circumference = π × diameter; π is approximately equal to 3.14.

VOLUME of a:

cube	Volume = edge^3
rectangular solid	Volume = length × width × height
square pyramid	Volume = $\frac{1}{3}$ × (base edge)^2 × height
cylinder	Volume = π × radius^2 × height; π is approximately equal to 3.14.
cone	Volume = $\frac{1}{3}$ × π × radius^2 × height; π is approximately equal to 3.14.

COORDINATE GEOMETRY

distance between points = ; $\sqrt{(x_2 - x_1)^2 + (y_2 - y_1)^2}$; (x_1, y_1) and (x_2, y_2) are two points in a plane.

slope of a line = $\frac{y_2 - y_1}{x_2 - x_1}$; (x_1, y_1) and (x_2, y_2) are two points on the line.

PYTHAGOREAN RELATIONSHIP

$a^2 + b^2 = c^2$; a and b are legs and c the hypotenuse of a right triangle.

MEASURES OF CENTRAL TENDENCY

mean = $\frac{x_1 + x_2 + ... + x_n}{n}$, where the x's are the values for which a mean is desired, and n is the total number of values for x.

median = the middle value of an odd number of _ordered_ scores, and halfway between the two middle values of an even number of _ordered_ scores.

SIMPLE INTEREST

interest = principal × rate × time

DISTANCE

distance = rate × time

TOTAL COST

total cost = (number of units) × (price per unit)

Mathematics Part I   5

Directions: You will have 23 minutes to complete questions 1–13. You may use your calculator with these questions only. Choose the one best answer to each question.

1. Kelly's goal is to average $25,000 per month in sales for the first three months of the year. Her sales for January and February are shown in the graph below.

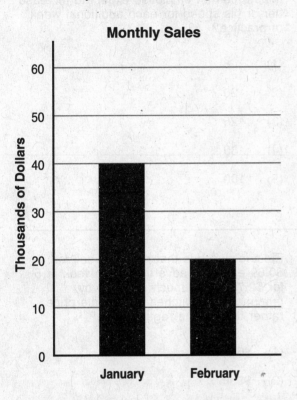

Monthly Sales

To reach her goal, what is the minimum amount of sales Kelly must make in March?

(1) $15,000

(2) $24,960

(3) $30,000

(4) $35,000

(5) $60,000

2. Ms. Nguyen is a real estate agent. One of her clients is considering buying a house in the Silver Lakes area, where 6 houses have recently sold for the following amounts: $160,000; $150,000; $185,000; $180,000; $145,000; $190,000. What should Ms. Nguyen report as the **MEDIAN** price of these houses?

(1) $160,000

(2) $170,000

(3) $180,000

(4) $190,000

(5) Not enough information is given.

3. If $3x - 6 = 12$, what is the value of x?

PLEASE DO NOT WRITE IN THIS TEST BOOKLET.

Mark your answer in the circles in the grid on your answer sheet.

GO ON TO THE NEXT PAGE

6   Mathematics Part I

<u>Questions 4 through 6</u> refer to the following graph and information.

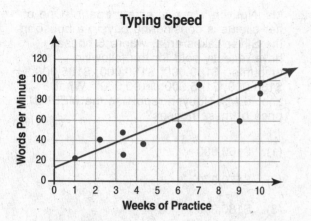

Typing Speed

Partners for Excellence offers its employees training classes to improve their typing skills. The graph above shows the typing speed results of 10 employees, as well as the line of best fit showing typing speed based on those results. The line of best fit can be used to make predictions for future employees who wish to take the classes.

4. What does the line of best fit predict the typing speed, in words per minute, will be for an employee who attends eight weeks of practice?

    PLEASE DO NOT WRITE IN THIS TEST BOOKLET.

    Mark your answer in the circles in the grid on your answer sheet.

5. Based on the line of best fit, what would be the approximate typing speed, in words per minute, of a person who had not practiced at all?

    (1)   0

    (2)   17

    (3)   20

    (4)   24

    (5)   29

6. The slope of the line of best fit represents the increase in words per minute for each additional week of practice. Based on the slope of the line, by how many words per minute can an employee expect to increase her or his speed for each additional week of practice?

    (1)   8

    (2)   20

    (3)   25

    (4)   80

    (5)   100

---

7. Electric switches that regularly sell for $0.69 each are advertised this week at 5 for $2.75. How much is saved by purchasing 5 switches at the sale price rather than at the regular price?

    (1) $6.20

    (2) $3.45

    (3) $2.75

    (4) $0.70

    (5) $0.14

GO ON TO THE NEXT PAGE

8. Leg XY of the right triangle shown in the diagram below is twice as long as leg YZ.

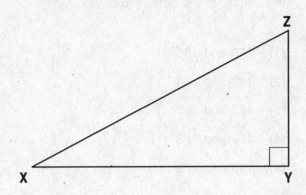

If the area of the triangle is 36 cm^2, what is the length, in cm, of leg XY?

(1)　6

(2)　9

(3)　12

(4)　18

(5)　24

9. The standard formula used by mechanics to find the length (L) of a fan belt of a car is as follows:

$$L = 2C + \frac{11(D + d)}{7} + \frac{(D - d)^2}{4C}$$

where D and d are the diameters of the wheels around which the belt runs, and C is the distance between the centers of the wheels.

What is L (in inches) if D = 12 inches, d = 2 inches, and C = 25 inches?

(1)　　39

(2)　　73

(3)　　97

(4)　　121

(5)　　229

10. Juanita had her car windshield replaced at a cost of $250. After a $50 deductible is applied (i.e., Juanita pays the first $50), her insurance company will pay 80 percent of the remaining balance. In dollars, how much will the insurance company pay?

PLEASE DO NOT WRITE IN THIS TEST BOOKLET.

Mark your answer in the circles in the grid on your answer sheet.

GO ON TO THE NEXT PAGE

11. The dimensions of the rectangle shown below are 2*x* and 3*x*.

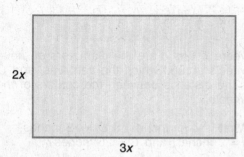

2*x*

3*x*

How many square units are in its area?

(1)   12

(2)   5*x*

(3)   10*x*

(4)   5*x*^{2}

(5)   6*x*^{2}

---

12. Susan left $650 in a savings account for one year. At the end of that time she received an interest credit of 5%. Then she withdrew all of her money and had to pay a service charge of $1.75. How much money did she have after paying the service charge?

(1) $648.25

(2) $653.25

(3) $680.75

(4) $682.50

(5) $684.25

13. The mean (average) weight of 5 boys is 160 pounds. If three of the boys weigh 152, 158, and 168 pounds respectively, which of the following could be the weights, in pounds, of the other two boys?

(1)   165 and 150

(2)   162 and 156

(3)   160 and 162

(4)   157 and 168

(5)   155 and 172

END OF MATHEMATICS PART I

Tests of
General Educational
Development

Mathematics

Official GED Practice Test

Calculator Use Not Allowed

GED Testing Service
American Council on Education

MATHEMATICS

Tests of General Educational Development

Directions

The Mathematics Test consists of multiple-choice questions intended to measure general mathematics skills and problem-solving ability. The questions are based on short readings that often include a graph, chart, or figure.

You will have 22 minutes to complete the 12 questions in this booklet. Work carefully, but do not spend too much time on any one question. Be sure you answer every question.

Formulas you may need are given on page 4. Only some of the questions will require you to use a formula. Not all the formulas given will be needed.

Some questions contain more information than you will need to solve the problem; other questions do not give enough information. If the question does not give enough information to solve the problem, the correct answer choice is "Not enough information is given."

The use of calculators is not allowed.

Do not write in this test booklet. The test administrator will give you blank paper for your calculations. Record your answers on the separate answer sheet provided. Be sure all information is properly recorded on the answer sheet.

To record your answers, fill in the numbered circle on the answer sheet that corresponds to the answer you select for each question in the test booklet.

FOR EXAMPLE:

If a grocery bill totaling $15.75 is paid with a $20.00 bill, how much change should be returned?

(1) $5.25
(2) $4.75
(3) $4.25
(4) $3.75
(5) $3.25

(On Answer Sheet)

① ② ● ④ ⑤

The correct answer is "$4.25"; therefore, answer space 3 would be marked on the answer sheet.

Do not rest the point of your pencil on the answer sheet while you are considering your answer. Make no stray or unnecessary marks. If you change an answer, erase your first mark completely. Mark only one answer space for each question; multiple answers will be scored as incorrect. Do not fold or crease your answer sheet. All test materials must be returned to the test administrator.

GO ON TO THE NEXT PAGE

Mathematics

Mixed numbers, such as $3\frac{1}{2}$, cannot be entered in the alternate format grid. Instead, represent them as decimal numbers (in this case, 3.5) or fractions (in this case, 7/2). No answer can be a negative number, such as -8.

To record your answer for an alternate format question

- begin in any column that will allow your answer to be entered;
- write your answer in the boxes on the top row;
- in the column beneath a fraction bar or decimal point (if any) and each number in your answer, fill in the bubble representing that character;
- leave blank any unused column.

EXAMPLE:

The scale on a map indicates that 1/2 inch represents an actual distance of 120 miles. In inches, how far apart on the map will two towns be if the actual distance between them is 180 miles?

The answer to the above example is 3/4, or 0.75, inches. A few examples of how the answer could be gridded are shown below.

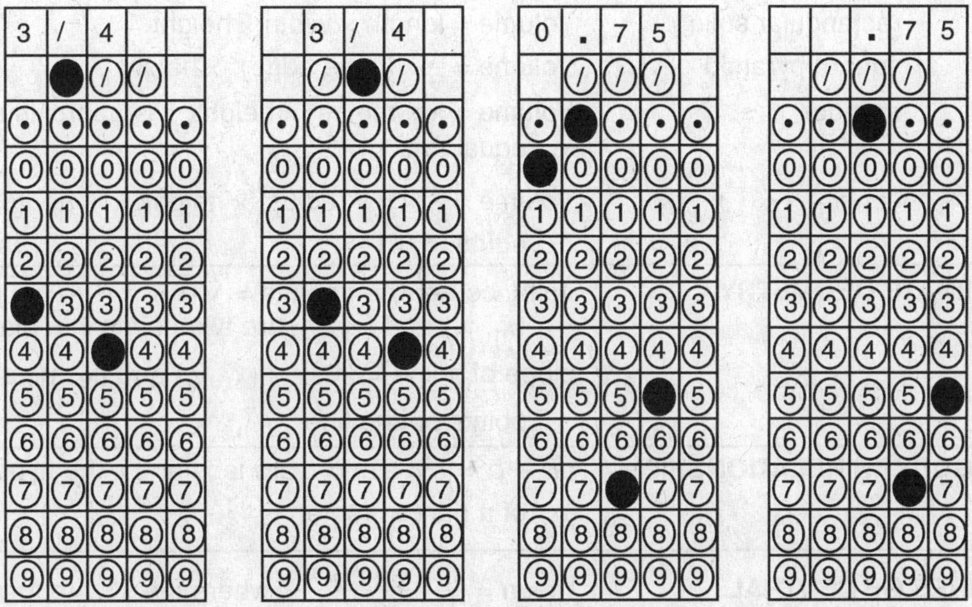

Points to remember:

- The answer sheet will be machine scored. **The circles must be filled in correctly.**
- Mark no more than one circle in any column.
- Grid only one answer even if there is more than one correct answer.
- Mixed numbers such as $3\frac{1}{2}$ must be gridded as 3.5 or 7/2.

Component: 9993949167
Kit: **ISBN 0-7398-5433-X**

DO NOT BEGIN TAKING THIS TEST UNTIL TOLD TO DO SO

4   **Mathematics**

FORMULAS

AREA of a:

square	Area = side^2
rectangle	Area = length × width
parallelogram	Area = base × height
triangle	Area = $\frac{1}{2}$ × base × height
trapezoid	Area = $\frac{1}{2}$ × (base$_1$ + base$_2$) × height
circle	Area = π × radius^2; π is approximately equal to 3.14.

PERIMETER of a:

square	Perimeter = 4 × side
rectangle	Perimeter = 2 × length + 2 × width
triangle	Perimeter = side$_1$ + side$_2$ + side$_3$

CIRCUMFERENCE of a circle   Circumference = π × diameter; π is approximately equal to 3.14.

VOLUME of a:

cube	Volume = edge^3
rectangular solid	Volume = length × width × height
square pyramid	Volume = $\frac{1}{3}$ × (base edge)^2 × height
cylinder	Volume = π × radius^2 × height; π is approximately equal to 3.14.
cone	Volume = $\frac{1}{3}$ × π × radius^2 × height; π is approximately equal to 3.14.

COORDINATE GEOMETRY   distance between points = $\sqrt{(x_2 - x_1)^2 + (y_2 - y_1)^2}$; (x_1, y_1) and (x_2, y_2) are two points in a plane.

slope of a line = $\frac{y_2 - y_1}{x_2 - x_1}$; (x_1, y_1) and (x_2, y_2) are two points on the line.

PYTHAGOREAN RELATIONSHIP $a^2 + b^2 = c^2$; a and b are legs and c the hypotenuse of a right triangle.

MEASURES OF CENTRAL TENDENCY   **mean** = $\frac{x_1 + x_2 + ... + x_n}{n}$, where the x's are the values for which a mean is desired, and n is the total number of values for x.

median = the middle value of an odd number of _ordered_ scores, and halfway between the two middle values of an even number of _ordered_ scores.

SIMPLE INTEREST   interest = principal × rate × time

DISTANCE   distance = rate × time

TOTAL COST   total cost = (number of units) × (price per unit)

Directions: You will have 22 minutes to complete questions 14–25. You may **NOT** use a calculator with these questions. Choose the one best answer to each question.

14. The scale on a hiker's map states that 1 inch = 2000 feet. Anna wants to know how far it is to her next campsite. On the map, the next campsite is 5 inches from her present location. What is the actual distance, in feet, between Anna's present location and her next campsite?

    (1)   5
    (2)   400
    (3)   600
    (4)   5,000
    (5)   10,000

15. The graph below shows the expected rainfall from a hurricane, based on the speed at which the hurricane is moving.

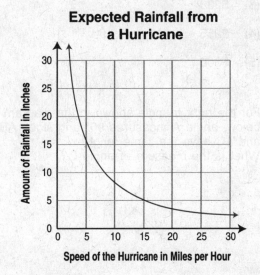

Expected Rainfall from a Hurricane

Based on the graph, what would be the approximate amount of rainfall, in inches, if a hurricane moves at 12 mph?

    (1)   15
    (2)   12
    (3)   10
    (4)   7
    (5)   4

GO ON TO THE NEXT PAGE

6   **Mathematics Part II**

16. A company charges $60 per day plus $0.50 per mile for truck rentals. If Greg rents a truck for 3 days and drives it a total of 150 miles, what will the company charge?

   (1) $110

   (2) $135

   (3) $230

   (4) $255

   (5) $300

17. For the right triangle shown in the diagram below, angle A measures 90° and sides AB and AC have the same length.
What is the measure of angle C?

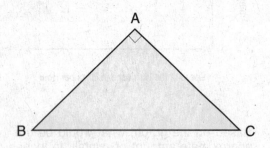

   (1)   30°

   (2)   45°

   (3)   60°

   (4)   90°

   (5)   135°

18. A carpenter is making a larger triangular brace similar to the one shown below.

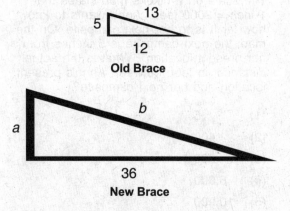

The base of the new brace is 36 inches. What is the length, in inches, of side b if the triangles are similar?

PLEASE DO NOT WRITE IN THIS TEST BOOKLET.

Mark your answer in the circles in the grid on your answer sheet.

_____

19. To rent a ball field for a game costs a $300 basic fee plus a $2 fee per person. If x persons attend the game, which equation can be used to find T, the total cost of renting the ball field?

   (1) $T = 2x + 300$

   (2) $T = 300x + 2$

   (3) $T = (300 + 2)x$

   (4) $T = \dfrac{300 + 2}{x}$

   (5) $T = (300)(2x)$

GO ON TO THE NEXT PAGE

<u>Questions 20 and 21</u> refer to the graph below.

Projected Cost and Revenue Functions For Solartex's Newest Computer Game

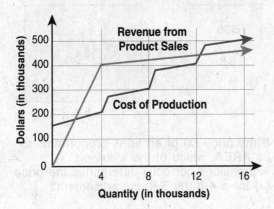

21. Based on market surveys, the cost of production is eventually projected to be greater than the revenue from sales. The graph shows this is likely to occur after approximately how many games have been produced?

    (1)   2,500

    (2)   4,500

    (3)   8,500

    (4)   10,500

    (5)   12,500

20. When none of the games has been sold, the revenue from sales will be zero. At the same time, the cost of production is expected to be approximately $150,000. Why might this be true?

    (1)   The game might not be popular at first.

    (2)   The price of the game might be too high at first.

    (3)   Start-up money must be spent to produce the games.

    (4)   The company may have decided to manufacture the game in small quantities at first.

    (5)   The game might sell better if it is introduced at a different time of year.

22. The graph of a circle is shown on the grid below.

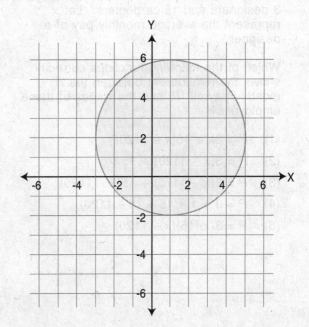

What point is the location of the center of the circle?

DO NOT MARK YOUR ANSWER ON THE GRAPH ABOVE.

Mark your answer on the coordinate plane grid on your answer sheet.

GO ON TO THE NEXT PAGE

23. Julio invested a sum of money at 6% interest. Krista invested $200 less than Julio, but her bank paid her 9% interest. After one year, what was the **DIFFERENCE** between the amount of interest Krista had earned and the amount of interest Julio had earned?

    (1) $ 6.00

    (2) $ 12.00

    (3) $ 18.00

    (4) $ 200.00

    (5) Not enough information is given.

24. Carpenters earn an average of $1120 less per month than designers at a furniture factory in Smithville. The factory employs 3 designers and 15 carpenters. Let x represent the average monthly pay of a designer.

    Which of the following functions correctly shows the relationship between the monthly payroll (P) and the wages of these employees?

    (1) $P = 3x + 15(x - 1120)$

    (2) $P = 3(x - 1120) + 15x$

    (3) $P = 3(x - 1120) + 15(x - 1120)$

    (4) $P = 3 + x + 15 + (x - 1120)$

    (5) $P = 3(x)(15)(x - 1120)$

25. The public transportation system in Central City charges $90 for a 2-ft. by 3-ft. rectangular advertising space in its buses.

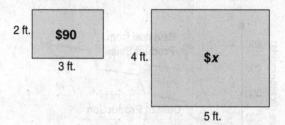

2 ft. | $90 | 3 ft.

4 ft. | $x | 5 ft.

If the price (x) of an ad is proportional to its **AREA,** which of the following expressions correctly determines the price (x) for a 4-ft. by 5-ft. advertisement?

(1) $\dfrac{5}{9} = \dfrac{90}{x}$

(2) $\dfrac{6}{20} = \dfrac{90}{x}$

(3) $\dfrac{6}{x} = \dfrac{20}{90}$

(4) $\dfrac{10}{18} = \dfrac{90}{x}$

(5) $\dfrac{10}{x} = \dfrac{18}{90}$

END OF EXAMINATION

To determine the standard score for the *Official GED Practice Tests Form PA: Mathematics Part I and Part II:*

1. Locate the number of questions the candidate answered correctly on the multiple-choice test.
2. Read the corresponding standard score from the column on the right.

Compare the candidate's standard scores to the minimum score requirements in the jurisdiction in which the GED credential is to be issued. (See *Appendix D* in the *Official GED Practice Tests Administrator's Manual.*)

U.S. Edition Form PA Mathematics	
Number of Correct Answers	Estimated GED Test Standard Score
25	800
24	690
23	610
22	550
21	520
20	500
19	480
18	470
17	450
16	440
15	440
14	430
13	420
12	410
11	400
10	390
9	380
8	370
7	360
6	340
5	320
4	290
3	250
2	210
1	200

Mathematics Part I Answers

1. 1
2. 2
3. 6 (or 6/1)
4. 80
5. 2
6. 1
7. 4
8. 3
9. 2
10. 160
11. 5
12. 3
13. 3

Mathematics Part II Answers

14. 5
15. 4
16. 4
17. 2
18. 39
19. 1
20. 3
21. 5
22. (1, 2)
23. 5
24. 1
25. 2

Pretest Answers and Solutions

1. (1) $\frac{x}{15} = \frac{50}{20}$

Set up a proportion that compares the ratio of the height of the tree (x) and the height of the dotted line to the distance between the left angle of the triangle and the tree and the distance between the left angle and the dotted line.

$$\frac{\text{tree height}}{\text{dotted line height}} = \frac{\text{distance from left angle to tree}}{\text{distance from left angle to dotted line}}$$

$$\frac{x}{15} = \frac{20 + 30}{20}$$

$$\frac{x}{15} = \frac{50}{20}$$

2. (4) 62.5

Set up a proportion and solve.

$$\frac{x}{15} = \frac{50}{20}$$

$$x = 50(15) \div 20$$

$$x = 750 \div 20 = 37.5$$

37.5 feet is the measure of one side of the right angle (the height of the tree), and $20 + 30 = 50$ feet is the measure of the other side.

Substitute $a = 37.5$ and $b = 50$ into the Pythagorean Theorem. Solve for c.

$$a^2 + b^2 = c^2$$

$$37.5^2\text{ ft} + 50^2\text{ ft} = c^2$$

$$1406.25\text{ ft}^2 + 2500\text{ ft}^2 = c^2$$

$$3906.25\text{ ft}^2 = c^2$$

$$c = \sqrt{3906.25\text{ ft}^2}$$

$$c = 62.5\text{ ft}$$

3. (4) $10\frac{1}{8}$

Convert all the distances to a common denominator of 8.

$$2\frac{3}{8} = 2\frac{3}{8}$$

$$3 = 3$$

$$1\frac{1}{2} = 1\frac{4}{8}$$

$$3\frac{1}{4} = 3\frac{2}{8}$$

Add all the distances along the route from Jackson back to Jackson.

$$2\frac{3}{8} + 3 + 1\frac{4}{8} + 3\frac{2}{8} = 9\frac{9}{8}$$

Convert the improper fraction.

$$9\frac{9}{8} = 10\frac{1}{8}$$

4. (1) (1, 0)

The x-coordinate in an ordered pair represents the number of spaces the point is located to the left or right of the origin. The origin is (0, 0). Point F is located one space to the right of the origin, so the x-coordinate is 1. The number is positive because it is located on the right side of the y-axis. The y-coordinate in an ordered pair represents the number of spaces the point is located above or below the x-axis. Since point F is located on the x-axis, the y-coordinate is 0. The ordered pair for point F is (1, 0).

5. (2) $\frac{1}{2}$

Substitute the coordinates into the equation for slope: $\frac{y_2 - y_1}{x_2 - x_1}$.

Point F (1, 0)

Point C (−3, −2)

$x_1 = 1$

$y_1 = 0$

$x_2 = -3$

$y_2 = -2$

$$\frac{-2 - 0}{-3 - 1} = \frac{-2}{-4} = \frac{1}{2}$$

6. (2) 19%

Subtract the number of calories in a serving of cereal without milk from the number of calories in a serving of cereal with milk.

$250 - 210 = 40$ calories

Find what percent 40 calories is of 210 calories by dividing.

$40 \div 210 \approx 0.19$

Convert the decimal to a percent by multiplying by 100 and adding a percent sign.

$0.19 \times 100 = 19\%$

7. (4) 2004 and 2005

Determine the increase from year to year. Choose the two years that had the greatest increase.

(1) From 2001 to 2002, the population increased from about 11,000 to about 13,000 for a total increase of 2,000.

(2) From 2002 to 2003, the population increased from about 13,000 to 20,000 for a total increase of 7,000.

(3) From 2003 to 2004, the population stayed the same; there was no increase.

(4) From 2004 to 2005, the population increased from about 20,000 to about 27,500 for a total increase of 7,500.

(5) From 2005 to 2006, the population increased from about 27,500 to about 29,000 for a total increase of 1,500.

The greatest increase in population was between the years 2004 and 2005.

8. (3) 2.35

Use the simple interest rate formula:

interest = principal × rate × time

Solve for time.

time = interest ÷ (principal × rate)

Convert the interest rate to a decimal: $4.75\% \div 100 = 0.0475$

Substitute the known values into the formula.

time = \$335 ÷ (\$3,000 × 0.0475)

time = \$335 ÷ (\$142.50) = 2.35 years

9. (2) $x < 7$

An open circle means that the number is not included in the inequality (no $\geq$ or $\leq$). Because the arrow is pointing to the left, the inequality indicates "less than," or $<$. The number line shows that the open circle starts on positive 7, so x is less than positive 7. This is represented by the inequality $x < 7$.

10. (1) 9:15 P.M.

Find the time that Sarah's class ends by adding 1 hour 45 minutes to 7:30 P.M., the time that the class begins.

First add hours.

7:30 P.M. + 1 hour = 8:30 P.M.

Split 45 minutes into smaller parts: 30 minutes and 15 minutes. Then count up by minutes to find the end time.

From 8:30 P.M. to 9:00 P.M. is 30 minutes.

From 9:00 P.M. to 9:15 P.M. is 15 minutes.

11. (5) Eduardo, Sarah, Keenan

Find a common denominator and compare.

Eduardo → $\frac{1}{4} = \frac{2}{8}$

Keenan → $\frac{3}{4} = \frac{6}{8}$

Sarah → $\frac{3}{8}$

$\frac{2}{8}, \frac{3}{8}, \frac{6}{8}$ = Eduardo, Sarah, Keenan

12. (5) ∠H

∠H has the same measure as ∠A because they are alternate exterior angles—two exterior angles on opposite sides of a line that bisects two parallel lines—which means they have the same measure. All the other answer options are angles that are supplementary to and smaller than ∠A.

13. (1) c = 18.50n

Chen will earn c dollars if he sells n aprons at $18.50 each. Translating the sentence, as written, into an equation yields $c = 18.50n$.

14. (1) 25°

∠CBE is an opposite angle to ∠DBA, so it is the same measure, 65°. ∠BCE is a right angle (as noted by the right angle symbol), so it measures 90°. The sum of the three interior angles of a triangle is 180°, so ∠CEB must measure $180° - 90° - 65° = 25°$.

15. (3) 41.5

First find the hypotenuse $\overline{BE}$ by using the Pythagorean Theorem.

Substitute $a = 14.6$ and $b = 9.5$ into the Pythagorean Theorem. Solve for c.

$a^2 + b^2 = c^2$

14.6^2 m $+ 9.5^2$ m $= c^2$

213.16 m$^2 + 90.25$ m$^2 = c^2$

303.4 m$^2 = c^2$

$c = \sqrt{303.4 \text{ m}^2}$

$c = 17.4$ m

Add the measurements of all three sides to find the perimeter.

17.4 m $+ 9.5$ m $+ 14.6$ m $= 41.5$ m

16. (1) $\frac{1}{4}$

Probability $= \dfrac{\text{number of favorable outcomes}}{\text{number of possible outcomes}}$

Probability $= \dfrac{\text{landing on E or F}}{\text{total sections}} = \dfrac{2}{8} = \dfrac{1}{4}$

17. (5) $3,150.00

Find the column in the chart that shows Age. Find 46 in that column. Move your finger horizontally to the right to the column labeled Annual Cost. Read 31.50. Remember that the column says, "Annual Cost per $1,000." Since Sally wants to buy $100,000 coverage, divide $100,000 by $1,000.

$100,000 \div 1,000 = 100$

Multiply $100 by the annual cost per $1,000 for a 46-year-old person ($31.50) to find the total amount Sally would pay for $100,000 of coverage for one year.

$100 \times 31.50 = 3,150.00$

18. (2) 2.0%

Subtract the annual cost per $1,000 of coverage at age 47 from the annual cost per $1,000 of coverage at age 48.

$33.50 - 32.85 = 0.65$

Find what percentage $0.65 is of $32.85 by dividing.

$0.65 \div 32.85 = 0.02$

Change to a percent by multiplying by 100 and adding a percent sign.

$0.02 \times 100 = 2\%$

19. (4) $2(x - 20) + 2x = 280$

Choose a variable to represent one quantity, and then write expressions to represent the other quantities.

width $= (x - 20)$

length $= x$

perimeter $= 280$ yards

Set up an equation in words to represent the problem. Remember that the perimeter is the sum of the measurements of all the sides. Use the formula for perimeter.

2 widths + 2 lengths = perimeter

Substitute the expressions into the word equation, and then solve.

$2(x - 20) + 2x = 280$

20. (4) Bad News Blues sold 65,000 files in August.

Option (4) is correct because the bar for Bad News Blues is halfway between 70 and 60 and the scale is in thousands of digital music files sold. Option (1) is incorrect because Bad News Blues outsold Swingin' by 20,000 digital files, which is less than 25,000. Option (2) is incorrect because River Boat Rock outsold Swingin' by 35,000 digital files, which is more than 3,500. Option (3) is incorrect because Swingin' sold 45,000 digital music files. Option (5) is incorrect because you would need to know the number of digital music files each group sold in July to be able to determine whether sales decreased or increased in August.

Answers and Solutions

Skill 1 Comparing and Ordering Numbers
Pages 12–13

1. (2) Juan, Tom, DeWayne

Convert the fractions to decimals by dividing, and then arrange from least to greatest.

Tom $1 \div 2 = 0.500$
Juan $1 \div 4 = 0.250$
DeWayne $5 \div 8 = 0.625$

2. (5) $0.25 each

Find the unit price for each tag by dividing the price by the quantity. Choose the smallest price

First tag $\$1.00 \div 3 = \$0.33$ each
Second tag $\$0.30$ each
Third tag $\$1.25 \div 4 = \$0.31$ each
Fourth tag $\$0.35$ each
Fifth tag $\$0.25$ each

3. (1) $\frac{2}{5}$

Think of the fractions as parts of a dollar Convert the fractions to decimals.

$\frac{2}{5} = \$0.40$

$\frac{2}{6} = \$0.33$

$\frac{3}{10} = \$0.30$

$\frac{2}{7} = \$0.29$

$\frac{3}{9} = \$0.33$

Then compare to the greatest price tag in the figure, which is $0.35. Only $\frac{2}{5}$ has a greater value.

4. (3) C and E

Switch books C (302.5) and E (301.5) so that the books are in the following order:
301.2, 301.23, 301.5, 301.9, 302.5

5. (2) Cedar

Write the ratios as division expressions, and calculate the student/teacher ratio.

Mina = 62 students ÷ 3 teachers = 20.67 students/teacher
Cedar = 74 students ÷ 4 teachers = 18.5 students/teacher
Fox = 47 students ÷ 2 teachers = 23.5 students/teacher
Rosewood = 26 students ÷ 1 teachers = 26 students/teacher
Travis = 51 students ÷ 2 teachers = 25.5 students/teacher
Cedar has the fewest students per teacher.

6. (3) Town D

Convert fractions to decimals and compare.

A to B = $7\frac{3}{4} = 7.75$

A to C = $7\frac{1}{2} = 7.50$

A to D = $7\frac{1}{3} = 7.33$

A to E = 8

A to F = $7\frac{7}{10} = 7.70$

7. (2) A→C→D→A

Convert the fractions to decimals. Add the round trip distances and compare. Choose the shortest route.
A to B to C to A = 7.75 + 10 + 7.5 = 25.25
A to C to D to A = 7.5 + 10 + 7.33 = 24.83
A to D to E to A = 7.33 + 10 + 8 = 25.33
A to E to F to A = 8 + 10 + 7.7 = 25.7

8. (4) Sofie, Melita, Roberta

Convert the numbers to a common form, such as decimal form.

Melita $\frac{5}{8} = 0.625$

Roberta $60\% = 0.600$

Sofie $\frac{2}{3} = 0.667$

9. (4) B and D

Convert the weights to a common form, such as decimal form. Choose the two greatest numbers.

A = 1.34 lb
B = $1\frac{1}{2}$ lb = 1.50 lb
C = $1\frac{1}{4}$ lb = 1.25 lb
D = 1.70 lb

10.

Convert the mixed numbers to improper fractions, and then divide to find the decimal equivalent. Add trailing zeros if needed. Compare the decimals. Choose the smallest weight.

$4\frac{5}{8} = \frac{37}{8} = 37 \div 8 = 4.6250$

$4\frac{7}{16} = \frac{71}{16} = 71 \div 16 = 4.4375$

$4.375 = 4.3750$

KEY Skill 2 Fractions and Mixed Numbers
Pages 16–17

1. (5) $\frac{7}{10}$

$\frac{3}{10} + \frac{1}{4} + \frac{3}{20}$

Find a common denominator and add. Then reduce the result to lowest terms.

$\frac{6}{20} + \frac{5}{20} + \frac{3}{20} = \frac{14}{20} \div \frac{2}{2} = \frac{7}{10}$

2. (3) $\frac{1}{10}$

$\frac{1}{5} - \frac{1}{10}$

$\frac{2}{10} - \frac{1}{10} = \frac{1}{10}$

3. (2) $14\frac{2}{2} - 6\frac{1}{2}$

Subtract the number of days skied, $6\frac{1}{2}$, from the total number of days on Joshua's ski pass, 15.

Change 15 to the improper fraction $14\frac{2}{2}$, so that the fractions have a common denominator and can be subtracted.

$14\frac{2}{2} - 6\frac{1}{2}$

4. (1) $2\frac{3}{4}$

8 hours − $5\frac{1}{4}$ hours

Convert both numbers to improper fractions, and then subtract. Convert the final answer to a proper fraction.

$\frac{32}{4}$ hours − $\frac{21}{4}$ hours = $\frac{11}{4}$ hours = $2\frac{3}{4}$ hours

5. (5) Not enough information is given.

You need to know the distance between the start of the riding trail and the river.

6. (4) Multiply $\frac{33}{4}$ by $\frac{1}{2}$.

Convert the total acres to an improper fraction, and then multiply by half.

$8\frac{1}{4} = \frac{33}{4}$

$\frac{33}{4} \times \frac{1}{2}$

7. (5) 58

Find a common denominator.

$4\frac{1}{4} = 4\frac{1}{4}$

$5\frac{4}{8} = 5\frac{2}{4}$

$8\frac{3}{4} = 8\frac{3}{4}$

$10\frac{1}{2} = 10\frac{2}{4}$

Add the whole number parts.

$4 + 5 + 8 + 10 = 27$ hours

Add the fraction parts. Reduce the sum to lowest terms.

$\frac{1}{4} + \frac{2}{4} + \frac{3}{4} + \frac{2}{4} = \frac{8}{4} = 2$ hours

Add the whole number sum and the fraction sum.

$27 + 2 = 29$ hours

Multiply by 2.

$29 \times 2 = 58$ hours

8. (3) $177

Multiply Samantha's hours by $12. Convert any mixed numbers to improper fractions before multiplying.

$4\frac{1}{4} \times \$12 = \frac{17}{4} \times \$12 = \frac{\$204}{4} = \$51/week$

Multiply David's hours by $12. Convert any mixed numbers to improper fractions before multiplying.

$10\frac{1}{2} \times \$12 = \frac{21}{2} \times \$12 = \frac{\$252}{2} = \$126/week$

Add David's and Samantha's weekly pay rate.

$\$51/week + \$126/week = \$177/week$

9. (3) $17\frac{1}{2}$

Multiply the width of each board by 5 boards.

$3\frac{1}{2} \times 5 = \frac{7}{2} \times 5 = \frac{35}{2} = 17\frac{1}{2}$

10.

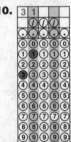

Since each board is 16 feet long, the total number of boards can be found by dividing 14 feet by the width of one board, $5\frac{1}{2}$ inches.

Convert 14 feet to inches.

14 feet × 12 inches = 168 inches

To divide 168 by $5\frac{1}{2}$, convert the mixed number to an improper fraction.

$168 \div 5\frac{1}{2} = 168 \div \frac{11}{2}$

Then invert the improper fraction and multiply across.

$\frac{168 \times 2}{1 \times 11} = \frac{336}{11} = 30.5$

Round up to a whole number.

Dayla needs 31 boards.

KEY Skill 3 Percents
Pages 20–21

1. (4) $3.50

Change the percent to a decimal.

10% ÷ 100 = 0.10

Find the part.

0.10 × $35 = $3.50

2. (5) 80%

Find the part.

$1200 ÷ $1500 = 0.80

Change to a percent.

0.80 × 100 = 80%

3. (3) 26,000(0.20)

Round the numbers.

25,978 ≈ 26,000

19% ≈ 20%

Convert the percent to a decimal.

20% ÷ 100 = 0.20

Choose the expression that shows the rounded number of votes (26,000) multiplied by the decimal (0.20).

4. (3) $4.12

Convert the sales tax percent to a decimal.

8.25% ÷ 100 = 0.0825

Multiply the decimal by the price of the music player.

0.0825 × $49.95 = $4.12

5. (1) $1200

$1500 is manufacturer cost (100%) plus 25%.

$1500 = 100% + 25% = 125%

Convert 125% to a decimal.

125 ÷ 100 = 1.25

Divide the base, 1500, by the rate, 1.25.

1500 ÷ 1.25 = 1200

6. (1) 86%

Find the percent as a decimal.

$3000 ÷ $3500 ≈ 0.86

Convert the decimal to a percent.

0.86 × 100 = 86%

7. (3) 3 ÷ 14 × 100

Round the subtotal of the bill.

$13.97 ≈ $14.00

Divide the tip by the subtotal.

$3 ÷ $14.00

Convert the decimal to a percent.

$3 ÷ $14.00 × 100

8. (4) $18.83

Add the cost of 1 additional orange juice to the original subtotal.

$13.97 + $1.99 = $15.96

Find the tip for the new subtotal.

$15.96 × 0.18 = $2.87

Add the new tip to the new subtotal.

$15.96 + $2.87 = $18.83

9. (2) 249 ÷ 1245 × 100

Find what percent 249 is of 1245 by dividing.

249 ÷ 1245

Convert to a percent.

249 ÷ 1245 × 100

10. (4) 54%

Find the rate by dividing.

135 ÷ 250 = 0.54

Convert the decimal to a percent.

0.54 × 100 = 54%

11.

Convert the percent to a decimal.

112% = 1.12

Multiply the decimal by the original value.

$32.50 × 1.12 = $36.40

KEY Skill 4 Ratio and Proportion
Pages 24–25

1. (4) 100

Convert the fraction in the scale to a decimal.

$\frac{1}{4}$ = 0.25 in.

Set up the proportion.

$\frac{\text{inches}}{\text{miles}} = \frac{0.25}{10} = \frac{2.5}{x}$

Find the cross product, and divide by the remaining term.

2.5 × 10 = 25

25 ÷ 0.25 = 100

2. (3) $0.93

Set up the proportion.

$\frac{6}{\$2.79} = \frac{2}{x}$

Find the cross product, and divide by the remaining term.

$2.79 × 2 = $5.58

$5.58 ÷ 6 = $0.93

3. (3) $\frac{13}{12}$

The number of shaded squares is 13.

The number of unshaded squares is 12.

4. (4) 1:1

Adding one more row would add 2 shaded squares and 3 unshaded squares.

The new number of shaded squares is 15.

The new number of unshaded squares is 15.

Reduce 15:15.

5. (1) 12

Set up the proportion.

$\frac{3}{4} = \frac{9}{x}$

Cross multiply, and then divide by the remaining term.

4 × 9 = 36

36 ÷ 3 = 12 = x

6. (1) $\frac{2.5}{2} = \frac{n}{3}$

Set up ratio of yards of fabric for 2 pillows.

$\frac{2.5 \text{ yards}}{2 \text{ pillows}}$

Set up ratio of n yards of fabric for 3 pillows.

$\frac{n \text{ yards}}{3 \text{ pillows}}$

Make a proportion by equating the two ratios.

$\frac{2.5}{2} = \frac{n}{3}$

7.

Set up the proportion.

$\frac{\text{hours}}{\text{dollars}} = \frac{25}{205} = \frac{35}{x}$

Find the cross product, and divide by the remaining term.

205 × 35 = 7,175

7,175 ÷ 25 = 287

8. (5) 3

Set up a proportion.

$\frac{\text{eggs}}{\text{days}} = \frac{8}{2} = \frac{12}{x}$

Find the cross product, and divide by the remaining term.

12 × 2 = 24

24 ÷ 8 = 3

9. (1) $\frac{3}{2} = \frac{900}{t}$

Set up a ratio of 900 adult tickets to an unknown number of children tickets.

$\frac{900}{t}$

Set up a proportion by equating the ratio with the unknown to $\frac{3}{2}$.

$\frac{3}{2} = \frac{900}{t}$

10. (3) 12.5

Set up a proportion.

$\frac{\text{squares}}{\text{inches}} = \frac{2}{5} = \frac{5}{x}$

Find the cross product, and divide by the remaining term.

5 × 5 = 25

25 ÷ 2 = 12.5

KEY Skill 5 Multi-Step Problems
Pages 28–29

1. (2) $285.78
$426.79 − $63.97 − $27.04 − $50.00

2. (5) 346(8.50) + 123(8.50 ÷ 2)
Multiply the ticket price for each show by the number of tickets sold. The ticket price for the evening show is $8.50.
Evening show: 346(8.50)
Tickets for the afternoon show sell for half that price.
Afternoon show: 123(8.50 ÷ 2)
Add the totals for the two shows.

3. (1) 25%
Add the number of cups of each ingredient to find the total number of cups of trail mix.
2.5 + 2 + 2 + 1.5 = 8 cups
Divide to find the percent of the mix that is raisins.
2 ÷ 8 = 0.25 = 25%

4. (3) 64%
Multiply length by width to find the areas of the two squares.
Smaller square area: 4 × 4 = 16
Larger square area: 5 × 5 = 25
Divide to find the percent of the larger square that is covered by the smaller square.
16 ÷ 25 = 0.64 = 64%

5. (4) 50%
Multiply length by width to find the area of the larger square.
Large square area: 5 × 5 = 25
Multiply $\frac{1}{2}$, or 0.5, base by height to find the area of the triangle.
Triangle area: 0.5(5)(5) = 12.5
Divide the area of the triangle by the area of the square to find the percent of the square that is covered by the triangle.
12.5 ÷ 25 = 0.5 = 50%

6. (4) 8 pounds
The sum of the parts given in the table equals 10, so each part is $\frac{1}{10}$, or 10% of the mix.
Sunflower seeds are 4 parts, or 40%, of the mix. Convert this number to a decimal.
40% = 0.40
Then multiply by 20 pounds to find the number of pounds of sunflower seeds in 20 pounds of mix.
0.40 × 20 = 8 pounds

7. (1) (0.10 + 0.20)30
The sum of the parts given in the table equals 10, so each part is $\frac{1}{10}$, or 10% of the mix.
Convert the parts for millet to decimals and then add.
0.10 + 0.20
Multiply the sum by 30 pounds.

8. (5) (480 − 400) ÷ 400 × 100
Enrique's salary increase: $480 − $400
Divide Enrique's salary increase by his original salary.
$80 ÷ $400
Multiply by 100 to convert to a percent.

9. (1) 5000 − 0.78(5000)
0.78(5000) represents the amount of the population who voted.
Subtract the amount that voted from the total population: 5000.

10.

Find the original discount.
30(0.30) = $9.00
First discounted price is $21.00.
Then find the additional discount using the new discounted price.
21(0.10) = $2.10
Final discounted price is $18.90.

11. (5) Not enough information is given.
You need to know the price of the radio.

KEY Skill 6 Tables and Charts
Pages 32–33

1. (5) Texas
Look at the 1990 column, and find the lowest number: $27,016. Find the state in the same row: Texas.

2. (3) Illinois
For each state, subtract the 1990 amount from the 2000 amount.
California $46,499 − $35,798 = $10,701
Florida $37,346 − $27,483 = $ 9,863
Illinois $45,606 − $32,252 = $13,354
Massachusetts $49,505 − $36,952 = $12,553
Texas $39,120 − $27,016 = $12,104
Illinois had the greatest increase: $13,354.

3. (3) $12,159
Subtract Florida's median income for 2000 from Massachusetts's median income for 2000.
$49,505 − $37,346 = $12,159

4. (4) $1270
Find the number in the *Income from EIC worksheet/But less than* column that is greater than $3154, which is 3200.
In the same row, find the corresponding EIC in the *Two Children* column ($1270).

5. (5) $798
Find $3000 in the *Income from EIC worksheet/At least* column. In the same row, find the EIC credit in the *No Children* column ($231) and the *One Child* column ($1029).
Then subtract.
$1029 − $231 = $798

6. (2) $1046
Find $3050 in the *Income from EIC worksheet/At least* column. In the same row find the EIC credit in the *One Child* column ($1046).

7. (4) 7747
Find June and July in the *Month* column. In the same rows add the corresponding number of visitors from the *Visitor* column.
3650 + 4097 = 7747

8. (5) $0.96

Subtract the least price from the greatest price in the *Detergent* column.

$6.45 − $5.49 = $0.96

9. (4) 6

Multiply: Serving Size × Servings per Container

$\frac{3}{4}$ cup × 8 servings = $\frac{24}{4}$ cups = 6 cups

10.

Multiply servings by calories.

3 servings × 250 calories = 750 calories

KEY Skill 7 Line Graphs
Pages 36–37

1. (2) $75

Find 1985 on the x-axis. Find the corresponding y-axis value. Since the point falls between two labels, add the labels and divide by 2.

($80 + $70) ÷ 2 = $75

2. (3) 1985 to 1990

1965 to 1970 = $38 − $32 = $6
1970 to 1975 = $45 − $38 = $7
1975 to 1980 = $55 − $45 = $10
1980 to 1985 = $75 − $55 = $20
1985 to 1990 = $103 − $75 = $28
1990 to 1995 = $122 − $103 = $19
1995 to 2000 = $148 − $122 = $26

3. (2) 21%

Find the difference in the food bill. $148 − $122 = $26
Divide the difference ($26) by the 1995 food bill to find the percent increase.

26 ÷ 122 = 0.21 = 21%

4. (4) 4 hours 25 minutes

Add the minutes spent doing homework each day.
30 + 50 + 40 + 60 + 45 + 0 + 40 = 265 minutes
Then divide by 60 minutes to find the mixed measure of time.
265 minutes ÷ 60 minutes = 4 hours 25 minutes

5. (4) Tuesday and Wednesday

Compare the times for each day.

Sunday	= 80
Monday	= 60
Tuesday	= 30
Wednesday	= 30
Thursday	= 50
Friday	= 0
Saturday	= 70

6. (5) Sunday

Find the days where the blue line is higher on the graph than the red line. Divide the total number of minutes spent watching television by the total number of minutes spent doing

---

homework. Choose the number that is more than 2 (twice).

Sunday	= 80 ÷ 30 ≈ 2.7 times more
Monday	= 60 ÷ 50 = 1.2 times more
Thursday	= 50 ÷ 45 ≈ 1.1 times more
Saturday	= 70 ÷ 40 = 1.75 times more

7. (5) 85°F

Compare the highest temperatures for each day.

Monday	= 80
Tuesday	= 85
Wednesday	= 75
Thursday	= 70
Friday	= 80
Saturday	= 80
Sunday	= 65

8. (1) Monday

Compare the difference in high and low temperatures for each day.

Monday	= 80 − 40 = 40
Tuesday	= 85 − 50 = 35
Wednesday	= 75 − 45 = 30
Thursday	= 70 − 55 = 15
Friday	= 80 − 60 = 20
Saturday	= 80 − 50 = 30
Sunday	= 65 − 60 = 5

9. (4) May and June

Find the monthly sales for each month. Choose the amounts greater than $4,000.

January	$1,500
February	$2,000
March	$2,000
April	$3,000
May	$4,500
June	$5,000

10. (2) $ 5,500

Add the sales for January, February, and March.
$1,500 + $2,000 + $2,000 = $5,500

11.

Find the difference in sales between May and March.
$4,500 − $2,000 = $2,500
Divide the difference ($2,500) by the March monthly sales ($2,000).
$2,500 ÷ $2,000 = 1.25 (or 125%)
Write the answer in decimal form.

KEY Skill 8 Bar and Circle Graphs
Pages 40–41

1. (3) 3.5

Subtract the number in 1960 from the number in 2000.
4.4 − 0.9 = 3.5

2. (3) 1970

Subtract to find each ten-year difference. Then compare and choose the greatest number.

1960 = 1.6 − 0.9 = 0.7
1970 = 2.3 − 1.4 = 0.9
1980 = 2.9 − 2.2 = 0.7
1990 = 3.8 − 3.0 = 0.8
2000 = 5.0 − 4.4 = 0.6

3. (4) 31%

Subtract to find the difference between the percent of the population aged 80 to 84 years in 1980 and in 1990.

3.8 − 2.9 = 0.9

Then divide this difference by the population that was aged 80 to 84 years in 1980 to find the percent increase.

0.9 ÷ 2.9 ≈ 0.31 = 31%

4. (4) 20%

Divide the amount Lana spends on her car by the total amount of her monthly income. Convert this number to a percent.

$275 ÷ $1350 ≈ 0.20 = 20%

5. (2) 1.5

Divide the amount spent on miscellaneous items by the amount spent on food.

$300 ÷ $200 = 1.5

6. (3) $\frac{150}{350}$

Place 150 in the top of the ratio and 350 in the bottom.

$\frac{150}{350}$

7. (3) 735

Convert 35% to a decimal.

35% = 0.35

Multiply the decimal by the total number of people to find the number of people who chose watching television.

2100 × 0.35 = 735

8.

Subtract to find the difference between the percent of people who chose reading and the percent who chose dining out.

18% − 15% = 3%

Convert this percent to a decimal.

3% = 0.03

Multiply the decimal by the total number of people surveyed to find how many more people chose reading than chose dining out.

0.03 × 2100 = 63

9. (3) Multiply 10% by 24, the number of hours in a day.

Change 10% to a decimal.

10% = 10 ÷ 100 = 0.10

Then multiply.

0.10 × 24 = 2.4

10. (2) $\frac{1}{4}$

Set up the percents as a ratio and reduce to lowest terms.

$\frac{20\%}{80\%} = \frac{2}{8} = \frac{1}{4}$

Skill 9 Probability
Pages 44–45

1. (4) $\frac{1}{2}$

Use the probability formula.

Probability = $\frac{\text{black sections}}{\text{yellow sections}} = \frac{1}{2}$

2. (4) $\frac{1}{5}$

Use the probability formula.

Probability = $\frac{\text{yellow sections}}{\text{total sections}} = \frac{2}{10} = \frac{1}{5}$

3. (3) $\frac{3}{5}$

Use the probability formula.

Probability = $\frac{\text{sections not green}}{\text{total sections}} = \frac{6}{10} = \frac{3}{5}$

4. (1) $\frac{1}{10}$

Use the probability formula.

Probability = $\frac{\text{black sections}}{\text{total sections}} = \frac{1}{10}$

5. (3) $\frac{(10 - 3)}{10}$

Use the probability formula.

Probability = $\frac{\text{total sections − red sections}}{\text{total sections}}$

6. (3) $\frac{3}{10} + \frac{4}{10}$

Probability of landing on green = $\frac{4}{10}$

Probability of landing on red = $\frac{3}{10}$

Add the probabilities.

7.

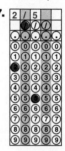

Find the sum of the colors. Then use the probability formula.

Probability = $\frac{6}{5 + 4 + 6} = \frac{6}{15} = \frac{2}{5}$

8. (5) Not enough information is given.

The specific number of students who wore gym pants is missing.

9. (3) $\frac{1}{6}$

Use the probability formula.

Probability = $\frac{\text{sides with 4}}{\text{total number of sides}} = \frac{1}{6}$

10. (1) Add the probability of rolling a 5 to the probability of rolling a 6.

You can find the probability of two outcomes by adding their probabilities.

11. (1) $\frac{1}{2}$

Use the probability formula.

Probability = $\frac{\text{sides with odd numbers}}{\text{total number of sides}} = \frac{3}{6} = \frac{1}{2}$

Pages 48–49

1. (5) 23

Calculate the elapsed time of Sorin's layovers between bus rides.

7:08 A.M. – 6:54 A.M. = 14 minutes

7:40 A.M. – 7:31 A.M. = 9 minutes

Add the layovers: 14 minutes + 9 minutes = 23 minutes

2. (2) 5:20

Read the time on the analog clock: 6:40

Subtract 1 hour 20 minutes from 6:40

6:40 – 1 hour 20 minutes = 5:20

3. (2) 1:25 P.M.

Add 4 hours 25 minutes to 9:00 A.M.

Add enough time to reach noon, and then add the remaining time.

9:00 A.M. + 3 hours = 12:00 P.M.

12:00 P.M. + 1 hour 25 minutes = 1:25 P.M.

4. (3) 4:55 P.M.

Add 1 hour and 10 minutes to 3:45 P.M., the end time of the first game.

3:45 P.M. + 1 hour 10 minutes = 4:55 P.M.

5. (5) 7 hours 35 minutes

Subtract 10:37 A.M. from 6:12 P.M.

Break the problem into two smaller problems, using 12:00 P.M. (noon) as a midpoint.

6:12 P.M. – 12:00 P.M. = 6 hours 12 minutes

12:00 P.M. – 10:37 A.M. = 1 hour 23 minutes

Add: 6 hours 12 minutes + 1 hour 23 minutes = 7 hours 35 minutes

6. (1) 11:30 A.M.

Divide to find the elapsed time.

90 orders ÷ 30 orders per hour = 3 hours

Add 3 hours to 8:30 A.M. to find the end time.

8:30 A.M. + 3 hours = 11:30 A.M.

7.

Subtract 9:45 P.M. from 5:15 A.M. (the next day).

Break the problem into two smaller problems, using 12:00 A.M. (midnight) as a midpoint.

5:15 A.M.– 12:00 A.M. = 5 hours 15 minutes

12:00 A.M. – 9:45 P.M. = 2 hours 15 minutes

Add: 2 hours 15 minutes + 5 hours 15 minutes = 7 hours 30 minutes

Convert 30 minutes to a decimal.

$30 \text{ minutes} \times \frac{1 \text{ hour}}{60 \text{ minutes}} = \frac{30 \text{ minutes}}{60 \text{ minutes}} = \frac{1}{2} = 0.5 \text{ hours}$

7 hours + 0.5 hours = 7.5 hours

8. (5) 7

Find the time Jennifer will end her break by adding 35 minutes to 1:00 P.M.

1:00 P.M. + 35 minutes = 1:35 P.M.

Each number on the clock represents 5 minutes, so 35 minutes ÷ 5 minutes = 7. The minute hand will point to the number 7 on the clock.

9. (3) 3 hours 45 minutes

Since Washington, D.C. is 2 hours ahead of Denver, subtract 2 hours from the Washington, D.C. time to have both times be in the same time zone as Denver.

5:05 P.M. – 2 hours = 3:05 P.M., arrival time in Washington, D.C.

To calculate the elapsed time of the flight, break the problem into two smaller problems using 12:00 P.M as a midpoint.

3:05 P.M.. – 12:00 P.M. = 3 hours 5 minutes

12:00 P.M. – 11:20 A.M.= 40 minutes

Add: 3 hours 5 minutes + 40 minutes = 3 hours 45 minutes

Pages 52–53

1. (3) 90° – 50°

Since ∠AFB and ∠BFC are complementary angles, the sum of their measures is 90°.

∠AFB + ∠BFC = 90°

Substitute for ∠AFB.

50° + ∠BFC = 90°

∠BFC = 90° – 50°

2. (5) Not enough information is given.

To solve for m∠2, you would subtract the sum of angles 3 and 4 from the sum of angles 2, 3, and 4, but the sum of angles 2, 3, and 4 is not given. This missing information is needed to solve.

3. (4) 180° – 90°

∠CFE and ∠CFA are supplementary, so ∠CFE + ∠CFA = 180°.

Substitute for ∠CFE.

90° + ∠CFA = 180°

∠CFA = 180° – 90°

4. (2) ∠4 measures 90°.

m∠1 is 90°, as shown by the right angle symbol. m∠4 is also 90° because it is a vertical angle, opposite to angle 1. Vertical angles have equal measures.

5.

∠1 = 90°

∠2 = Less than 90°

∠3 = Less than 90°

∠4 = 90°

∠5 = Less than 90°

∠6 = Less than 90°

There are 4 acute angles.

6. (4) They are vertical, or opposite, angles.

(1) No – they are vertex to vertex.

(2) No – they are both greater than 90º.

(3) No – they are both greater than 90º.

(4) Yes – they are vertical angles, which means they are congruent and have equal measures.

(5) This is true but does not address equal measures.

7. (3) ∠5 and ∠4

Angles 5 and 4 have the same measure because they are alternate exterior angles–two exterior angles on opposite sides of a line that bisects two parallel lines. Options (1), (2), (3), and (5) do not have equal angles because they are not opposite angles.

8. (4) 135°

Because the two lines are parallel to the horizontal line, ∠1 = ∠3 and ∠2 = ∠4.

Angles 1 and 2 are supplementary.

∠1 + ∠2 = 180°

Substitute for ∠1.

∠3 + ∠2 = 180°

∠3 = 180° − ∠2

Substitute for ∠2.

∠3 = 180° − 45° = 135°

9. (3) 48°

The problem states that two angles add to 90°

Set up an expression using A and B to show that seven times a number plus eight times the same number equals 90°. Let ∠A = 7x and ∠B = 8x.

∠A + ∠B = 90°

7x + 8x = 90°

Solve for x.

15x = 90°, $x = \frac{90°}{15} = 6$

Substitute for x. Choose the larger angle.

∠A = 7x = 7(6°) = 42°

∠B = 8x = 8(6°) = 48°

10. (3) 105°

∠ACB and ∠DCE are vertical angles. Vertical angles are opposite and equal.

Since ∠DCE = 105° and ∠DCE = ∠ACB, ∠ACB = 105°.

KEY **Skill 12** **Triangles**

Pages 55–57

1. (4) Triangle ADB is a right triangle.

Triangle ADB (option 4) is a right triangle because it has two perpendicular sides. There is not enough information to determine if triangle ABC (option 1) is a right triangle. Triangles BCD (option 2) and ABD (option 3) are right triangles. Triangle BDC (option 5) is not an isosceles triangle because it does not have two equal sides.

2. (2) 2

Perpendicular lines form right angles, so there are two right triangles: ABD and BCD.

3. (2) 45°

Write an equation: ∠A + ∠B + 90° = 180°

Since there are two equal angles, substitute for ∠B:

∠A + ∠A + 90° = 2∠A + 90° = 180°

Solve for ∠A: ∠A = (180° − 90°) ÷ 2 = 45°

4. (4) EFD and AFB

(1) AFB is obtuse and AFC is right.

(2) AFC is right and EFB is obtuse.

(3) DFC is right and BEF is obtuse.

(4) EFD is obtuse and AFB is obtuse.

(5) AFE is obtuse and AFC is right.

5.

Since ∠FAE and ∠FEA have equal measure, let x = ∠FAE = ∠FEA.

Write an equation: 2x + 96° = 180°.

Solve for x:

x = (180° − 96°) ÷ 2 = 84° ÷ 2 = 42° = ∠FEA

6. (5) 10

There are 10 triangles: AFB, AFC, AFD, AFE, BFC, BFD, BFE, CFD, CFE, and DFE.

7. (4) 4

There are 4 isosceles triangles: AEC, AEB, BED, and CED.

8. (2) $\frac{(180° - 90°)}{2}$

The triangle has 2 equal angles and 1 angle that is 90°. This means ∠C = ∠A.

Write an equation, and let x = ∠C = ∠A.

2x + 90° = 180°

Solve for x: x = (180° − 90°) ÷ 2

9. (1) right

When two sides of a triangle are perpendicular, the triangle is a right triangle. All four triangles formed in the figure have two perpendicular sides, so they are all right triangles.

10. (2) 70°

If $\overline{AD}$ is congruent to $\overline{CD}$, then ∠CAD = ∠ACD.

Since ∠CAD is 55°, ∠ACD is also 55°.

The sum of the angles of a triangle is 180°.

Write an equation and let x = ∠ADC.

180° − ∠CAD − ∠ACD = x

Substitute and solve for x.

180° − 55° − 55° = x = 70° = ∠ADC

11. (3) 12

If $m∠BAC$ = $m∠BCA$, then $\overline{CB}$ = $\overline{AB}$.

Substitute the known length of $\overline{CB}$.

12 in. = $\overline{AB}$

Skill 13 **Pythagorean Theorem**

Pages 60–61

1. (4) $\sqrt{7^2 + 10^2}$

Substitute a = 7 and b = 10 into the Pythagorean Theorem. Solve for c without calculating the squares.

$a^2 + b^2 = c^2$

7^2 cm + 10^2 cm = c^2

$c = \sqrt{7^2 \text{cm} + 10^2 \text{cm}}$

2. (2) 10

Substitute b = 24 and c = 26 into the Pythagorean Theorem. Solve for a.

$a^2 + b^2 = c^2$

$a^2 + 24^2$ ft = 26^2 ft

$a^2 + 576$ ft = 676 ft

$a^2 = 100$ ft
$a = \sqrt{100}$ ft
$a = 10$ ft

3. (2) 2 and 3

Substitute $a = 1$ and $c = 3$ into the Pythagorean Theorem. Solve for b.

$a^2 + b^2 = c^2$
1^2 m $+ b^2$ m $= 3^2$ m
$b^2 = 3^2$ m $- 1^2$ m
$b^2 = 9$ m $- 1$ m $= 8$ m
$b = \sqrt{8}$ m

The measurement of b will be between 2 meters and 3 meters. The square root of 4 meters is 2 meters and the square root of 9 meters is 3 meters. Therefore, the square root of any number between 4 meters and 9 meters must be between 2 meters and 3 meters.

4. (5) Not enough information is given.

This problem should be solved using the Pythagorean Theorem. However, the height of the tower between the ground and the point at which the cables are attached needs to be known. To find that distance, the height of the tower must be known.

5. (5) 50

Use the Pythagorean Theorem.

Let $a = 40$ feet (the distance between the top of the cable and the ground).

Let $b = 30$ feet (the distance between the tower and the bottom of the cable).

Let $c =$ the length of the cable.

Solve for c.

$a^2 + b^2 = c^2$
40^2 feet $+ 30^2$ feet $= c^2$
1600 feet $+ 900$ feet $= c^2$
$c^2 = 2500$ feet
$c = \sqrt{2500}$ feet
$c = 50$ feet

6. (3) Use the Pythagorean Theorem. Let $a = 24$ miles and $b = 18$ miles. Solve for c.

Use the Pythagorean Theorem.

$a^2 + b^2 = c^2$

Let $a = 24$ miles (the distance between Carson and Bethel).

Let $b = 18$ miles (the distance between Athens and Carson).

Let $c =$ the distance between Bethel and Athens.

Solve for c.

7. (4) $\sqrt{425} + 3$

Use the Pythagorean Theorem.

Let $a = 20$ (building height).

Let $b = \frac{1}{4}$ of 20, or 5 (the ground distance from the tower).

Let $c =$ the length of the ladder minus 3.

Solve for c.

$a^2 + b^2 = c^2$
$20^2 + 5^2 = c^2$
$400 + 25 = c^2$
$c^2 = 425$

Add 3 for the distance ladder extension above the roof.

$c = \sqrt{425} + 3$

8.

Use the Pythagorean Theorem.

Let $a = 1$ ft $= 12$ in. (post length).

Let $b = 16$ in. (length of the mailbox).

Let $c =$ length of the diagonal brace.

Solve for c.

$a^2 + b^2 = c^2$
12^2 in. $+ 16^2$ in. $= c^2$
144 in. $+ 256$ in. $= c^2$
$c^2 = 400$ in.
$c = \sqrt{400}$ in.
$c = 20$ in.

9. (1) 40

Use the Pythagorean Theorem.

The distance between Gate C and Gate B is twice the distance from Gate A to the center ($2 \times 25 = 50$).

Let $a =$ distance from Gate A to Gate B.

Let $b = 30$ yd (distance from Gate A to Gate C).

Let $c = 50$ yd (distance from Gate C to Gate B).

Solve for c.

$a^2 + b^2 = c^2$
$a^2 + 30^2$ yd $= 50^2$ yd
$a^2 = 50^2$ yd $- 30^2$ yd
$a^2 = 2500$ yd $- 900$ yd
$a^2 = 1600$ yd
$a = \sqrt{1600}$ yd
$a = 40$ yd

Skill 14 Perimeter, Area, and Volume
Pages 64–65

1. (3) 2(9) + 2(12)

Perimeter is the distance around.

Use the perimeter formula for a rectangle:

perimeter $= 2 \times$ length $+ 2 \times$ width

Substitute the known values.

perimeter $= 2(9) + 2(12)$

2. (2) 22.5

Convert all the known values to the same units:

6 in. $= 0.5$ ft

Use the volume formula for a rectangular solid:

volume $=$ length $\times$ width $\times$ height

Substitute the known values.

volume $= 15$ ft $\times 3$ ft $\times 0.5$ ft

volume $= 22.5$ cubic ft

3. (1) 3.14(9)(2)

Use the volume formula for a cylinder:

$\pi \times$ radius$^2 \times$ height

Substitute the known values.

volume $= \pi \times (3$ ft$)^2 \times 2$ ft

Simplify. Use 3.14 for π.
volume = 3.14 × 9 ft² × 2 ft

4. **(3) 6 × 6**

Convert the size of the squares from inches to feet:
12 in. = 1 ft. Each square is 1 ft by 1 ft.
Use the area formula for a rectangle to find the area of one square.
area of square = side²
area of one square = 1 ft × 1 ft = 1 ft²
Since the area of each square is 1 ft² and the quilt is square, the sides of the quilt will have equal measurements.
Choose the answer choice that multiplies the square of 36 ft² times itself.
6 ft × 6 ft = 36 ft²

5. **(5) (20)(15)(1.5) ÷ 27**

Use the volume formula for a rectangular solid:
volume = length × width × height
Substitute the known values:
volume = 20 ft × 15 ft × 1.5 ft = (20)(15)(1.5)
Divide by the number of cubic feet in a yard (27).
volume in cubic yards = (20)(15)(1.5) ÷ 27

6. **(3) 18.84**

Use the formula for circumference of a circle:
circumference = π × diameter
Substitute the known values.
circumference = π × 6 yards = 3.14 × 6 yards = 18.84 yards

7. **(4) 4225**

Use the area formula for a trapezoid:
area = $\frac{1}{2}$ × (base₁ + base₂) × height
Substitute the known values:
area = $\frac{1}{2}$ × (50 ft + 80 ft) × 65 ft
Simplify: area = $\frac{1}{2}$ × (130 ft) × 65 ft = 8450 ft² ÷ 2
area = 4225 ft²

8. **(2) $\frac{1}{2}$ × (50 + 80) × 65 + (32 × 80)**

Use the area formula for a trapezoid:
area = $\frac{1}{2}$ × (base₁ + base₂) × height
Substitute the known values:
area = $\frac{1}{2}$ × (50 ft + 80 ft) × 65 ft
Use the area formula for a rectangle: area = length × width
Substitute the known values.
area = 80 ft × 32 ft
Add the two areas together.
Total area = trapezoid area + rectangle area
Total area = $\frac{1}{2}$ × (50 ft + 80 ft) × 65 ft + (80 ft × 32 ft)

9. **(2) 1,000**

Use the area formula for a square: area = side²
The area of one 12-inch square is 1 ft².
Find the area of the greenhouse floor.
Use the area formula for a rectangle:
area = length × width
Substitute the known values.
area = 40 ft × 25 ft = 1000 ft²
Divide by the area of one tile:
1000 ft² ÷ 1 ft² = 1000 tiles

10. **(3) 9 inches**

Use the volume formula for a rectangular solid:
volume = length × width × height
Substitute the known values.
30 ft³ = 8 ft × 5 ft × height = 40 ft² × height

Divide: height = 30 ft³ ÷ 40 ft² = 0.75
Convert to inches: 12 in. = 1 ft
Set up a proportion: $\frac{12 \text{ in.}}{1 \text{ ft}} = \frac{x}{0.75 \text{ ft}}$
Cross multiply and solve for x.
x(1 ft) = (12 in.)(0.75 ft)
x = (12 in.)(0.75 ft) ÷ 1 ft
x = 9 in.

11. **(3) 150**

Find the length of the missing sides. The length of the top side is 30 m + 15 m, or 45 m. The length of the missing bottom right side is 30 m − 15 m, or 15 m. Add all the sides:
30 + 30 + 15 + 15 + 15 + 45 = 150.

12.

Use the area formula for a triangle:
area = $\frac{1}{2}$ × base × height
Substitute the known values: area = $\frac{1}{2}$ × 15 m × 15 m
Simplify: area = $\frac{1}{2}$ × 225 m² = 225 m² ÷ 2
area = 112.5 m²

Skill 15 Coordinates
Pages 68–69

1. **(1) (4, −2)**

From point B, follow a vertical line until you reach the x-axis. This is the x-coordinate (4). Then, from point B again, follow the horizontal line until you reach the y-axis. This is the y-coordinate (−2). The ordered pair for point B is (4, −2).

2. **(5) F**

Start at the origin (0, 0). Move 1 unit to the right along the x-axis. Move right because the number is positive. Then move 0 units along the y-axis. Point F is located at (1, 0).

3. **(4) E**

Start at the origin (0, 0). Move 3 units to the left along the x-axis. Move left because the number is negative. Then move 2 units up along the y-axis. Move up because the number is positive. Point E is located at (−3, 2).

4. **(2) (−3, 0)**

Point E is on the x-axis. This is the x-coordinate (−3). Since point E is on the x-axis, the y-coordinate is 0. The ordered pair for point E is (−3, 0).

5. **(1) A**

Start at the origin (0, 0). Move 1 unit to the left along the x-axis. Move left because the number is negative. Then move 2 units up along the y-axis. Move up because the number is positive. Point A is located at (−1, 2).

6. **(4) From the origin, move 2 units to the right.**

Start with the x-coordinate. Move right along the x-axis because the number is positive. Move 2 units because the x-coordinate is 2.

7. **(3) B and F**

Find the coordinates for all the points.

$A = (-1, 2)$
$B = (2, 4)$
$C = (4, 2)$
$D = (-4, -2)$
$E = (-3, 0)$
$F = (2, -1)$
Points *B* and *F* have the same *x*-coordinate because the first number in each ordered pair is 2.

8. (3) (–1, –5)
From point *A*, follow a vertical line until you reach the *x*-axis. This is the *x*-coordinate (–1). Then, from point *A* again, follow the horizontal line until you reach the *y*-axis. This is the *y*-coordinate (–5). The ordered pair for point *A* is (–1, –5).

9. (4) F
Find the coordinates for all the points in the answer choices.
$C = (-1, 4)$
$D = (3, 3)$
$E = (-4, 1)$
$F = (4, -3)$
Point *F* is the only point with a greater *x*-value than *y*-value.

10. (3) C
Start at the origin (0, 0). Move 1 unit to the left along the *x*-axis. Move left because the number is negative. Then move 4 units up along the *y*-axis. Move up because the number is positive. Point *C* is located at (–1, 4).

11.

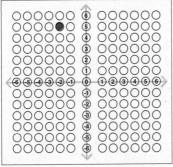

Start at the origin (0, 0). Move 2 units to the left along the *x*-axis. Move left because the number is negative. Then move 5 units up along the *y*-axis. Move up because the number is positive.

12.

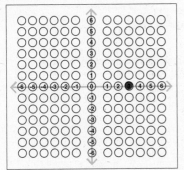

Start at the origin (0, 0). Move 3 units to the right along the *x*-axis. Move right because the number is positive. Then move 0 units along the *y*-axis.

1. (3) 71
Substitute for *x*.
$3(5)^2 - 4$
$3(25) - 4$
$75 - 4 = 71$

2. (1) three less than two times a number equals seven
The phrase "three less" means "to subtract 3," or –3.
The phrase "two times a number" means multiply by 2, or 2*x*.
$2x - 3 = 7$ means three less than two times a number equals seven.

3. (3) x ≥ –3
The number line shows that point x is equal to or greater than –3. This is shown by the inequality x ≥ –3.

4. (5) $\frac{1}{3}$
Substitute for *x* and *y*. Reduce.
$\frac{x}{y} = \frac{3}{9} = \frac{1}{3}$

5. (1) 7
Substitute for *q*.
$p = 4(7 - 7) + 7$
$p = 4(0) + 7$
$p = 0 + 7$

6. (2) a < 2
Subtract 6 from each side.
$2a + 6 - 6 < 10 - 6$
$2a < 4$
Divide by 2.
$\frac{2a}{2} < \frac{4}{2}$
$a < 2$

7. (1) w = 4
Substitute for *l* and *A*.
$34 = (8.5)w$
Divide both sides by 8.5.
$\frac{34}{8.5} = \frac{8.5w}{8.5}$
$w = 4$

8. (4) 20
Substitute for *a* and *b*.
$7(2) - 3(-2)$
$14 + 6$
20

9.

Subtract 8 from both sides.
$\frac{n}{4} + 8 - 8 = 12 - 8$
$\frac{n}{4} = 4$

Multiply both sides by 4.

$\frac{n}{4} \times 4 = 4 \times 4$

$n = 16$

10. (3) P = 56

Substitute for l and w.

$P = 2(16) + 2(12)$

$P = 32 + 24$

$P = 56$

11. (3) $4^2 + 8 = 6 - 3$

Eight more means add 8.

The square of four means 4^2.

"Is the same" means "equals."

Three less than six means $6 - 3$.

Eight more than the square of four is the same as three less than six is represented by $4^2 + 8 = 6 - 3$.

12. (1) −1

Divide each side of the inequality by 6 to isolate the variable. Remember to reduce your result to lowest terms.

$\frac{6z}{6} < \frac{-3}{6}$

$z < \frac{-1}{3}$

Find the answer choice that satisfies the inequality.

$-1 < \frac{-1}{3}$

13. (2) 159

Substitute for r and s.

$3(7)^2 - 4(-3)$

$3(49) - (-12)$

$147 + 12$

159

14. (2) d = 21

Substitute for C and π.

$66 = \frac{22}{7} d$

$66 \times 7 = 22d$

$462 = 22d$

$462 \div 22 = d = 21$

15. (5)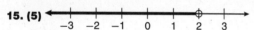

Divide each side by 3 and simplify.

$\frac{3x}{3} < \frac{6}{3}$

$x < 2$

The equation is represented by an empty circle on 2 with an arrow extending left to represent all values less than 2.

16.

Substitute for z and x. Solve for y.

$y = 5(2)(-4 + 7)$

$y = 5(2)(3)$

$y = (10)3$

$y = 30$

122 *Keys to GED® Success: Mathematics*

KEY Skill 17 Linear Equations

Pages 76–77

1. (2) $\frac{-4 - 3}{2 - (-3)}$

Substitute the coordinates into the equation for slope.

$x_1 = -3$

$y_1 = 3$

$x_2 = 2$

$y_2 = -4$

$\frac{-4 - 3}{2 - (-3)}$

2. (3) $\frac{1}{3}$

Substitute the coordinates into the equation for slope.

$x_1 = 4$

$y_1 = 1$

$x_2 = -5$

$y_2 = -2$

$\frac{-2 - 1}{-5 - 4} = \frac{-3}{-9} = \frac{1}{3}$

3. (3) $\frac{2 - (-3)}{2 - (-3)}$

Substitute the coordinates into the equation for slope.

$x_1 = -3$

$y_1 = -3$

$x_2 = 2$

$y_2 = 2$

$\frac{2 - (-3)}{2 - (-3)}$

4. (2) 0

Any line parallel to Line 2 will have the same slope as Line 2. As soon as you know the slope of Line 2, you will know the slope of any line parallel to it.

Substitute the known coordinates for Line 2 into the equation for slope.

$x_1 = -4$

$y_1 = 2$

$x_2 = 2$

$y_2 = 2$

$\frac{2 - 2}{2 - 4} = \frac{0}{-2} = 0$

Any line parallel to Line 2 will have a slope of 0.

5. (3) (0, 2)

The y-intercept is the point at which the line crosses the y-axis.

Line 2 crosses the y-axis at (0, 2).

6. (4) $\frac{5}{2}$

Substitute the coordinates into the equation for slope.

$x_1 = 4$

$y_1 = 1$

$x_2 = 2$

$y_2 = -4$

$\frac{-4 - 1}{2 - 4} = \frac{-5}{-2} = \frac{5}{2}$

7. (4) (2, 1)

For a point to exist on two separate lines, the lines must cross. The common point is the intersection of the lines.

The intersection of the two lines shown on the graph is (2, 1).

8. (5) y = 2x − 3

Input two different x-values of two known ordered pairs to check which equation yields the correct y-values.

Two points on Line 2 are (2, 1) (the intersection of the lines) and $(0, -3)$, the y-intercept.

Substituting 2 into the equations needs to yield 1 for $(2, 1)$ to be on Line 2.

(1) No; $y = -3(2) + 2 = -6 + 2 = -4$

(2) No; $y = -2(2) + 3 = -4 + 3 = -1$

(3) No; $y = \frac{1}{2}(2) + 2 = 1 + 2 = 3$

(4) No; $y = 2 + 2 = 4$

(5) Yes; $y = 2(2) - 3 = 4 - 3 = 1$

Option (5) is the only equation that yields the correct y value. Now check that the other point works.

Substituting 0 into the equation needs to yield -3 for $(0, -3)$ to be on Line 2.

$y = 2(0) - 3 = -3$

Because both points are on the line, option 5 is the linear equation for Line 2.

9. (4) $\frac{3}{5}$

Substitute the coordinates into the equation for slope.

$x_1 = 0$

$y_1 = 0$

$x_2 = 5$

$y_2 = 3$

$\frac{3 - 0}{5 - 0} = \frac{3}{5}$

10. (3) $y = \frac{-1}{2}x + 1$

Use the equation for slope-intercept form, where m is slope and b is the y-intercept.

$y = mx + b$

Find the equations with the same slope as the equation in the question, $y = \frac{-1}{2}x - 1$.

slope $= \frac{-1}{2}$

y-intercept $= -1$

The linear equation $y = \frac{-1}{2}x + 1$ (option 3) is parallel because it has the same slope $\left(\frac{-1}{2}\right)$ and a different y-intercept (1).

11.

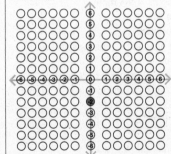

Rearrange the equation to be in the form $y = mx + b$.

Subtract 4x from both sides.

$-4x + 4x + y = -4x + (-2)$

$y = -4x + (-2)$

The y-intercept is in the form $(0, b)$.

The y-intercept is $(0, -2)$.

KEY Skill 18 Functions

Pages 80–81

1. (3) 5

Substitute known value of x in the equation, and solve for y.

$y = 4x - 3$

$y = 4(2) - 3$

$y = 8 - 3$

$y = 5$

2. (5) 1152

Use the equation for indirect variation.

$y = \frac{k}{x}$

Solve for the constant of variation, k.

$k = yx$

Substitute for y and x.

$k = (24)(48)$

$k = 1152$

3. (1) $18.50

$c = \$19.98$

Substitute for c in the equation. Solve for p.

$c = 1.08p$

$p = c \div 1.08$

$p = \$19.98 \div 1.08$

$p = \$18.50$

4. (4) 100,000

Substitute for t.

$p = 10^5$

$p = 10 \times 10 \times 10 \times 10 \times 10 = 100,000$

5. (5) indirect variation

An indirect variation is a function in which a constant is divided by one variable to find the other variable.

The 200 coats can be divided by the number of volunteers to find the number of deliveries.

6. (4) 64

Substitute for x to find the answer choice that is not a whole number.

(1) $y = 18 \div 6 = 3$

(2) $y = 36 \div 6 = 6$

(3) $y = 48 \div 6 = 8$

(4) $y = 64 \div 6 = 10\frac{4}{6}$, or $10\frac{2}{3}$

(5) $y = 66 \div 6 = 11$

7. (4) 81

Substitute for x to solve for y.

$y = 3^4$

$y = 3 \times 3 \times 3 \times 3 = 9 \times 9 = 81$

8. (3) $y = x + 2$

Substitute x values into the equations to see whether the function holds true.

Start by substituting $x = 3$ (which should yield $y = 5$, according to the figure).

(1) No; $y = 2x + 1 = 2(3) + 1 = 6 + 1 = 7$

(2) No; $y = x + 1 = 3 + 1 = 4$

(3) Yes; $y = x + 2 = 3 + 2 = 5$

(4) No; $y = x - 2 = 3 - 2 = 1$

(5) No; $y = 2x - 2 = 2(3) - 2 = 6 - 2 = 4$

Option 3 yields 5. Substitute another value of x to make sure the function is true.

Check $x = 2$ (which should yield $y = 4$, according to the figure).

$y = x + 2 = 2 + 2 = 4$

The equation $y = x + 2$ is true.

9. (2) 7

The function is based on a pattern of adding 2 to the x value in each column.

$2 + 1 = 3$ blocks

$2 + 2 = 4$ blocks

2 + 3 = 5 blocks
2 + 4 = 6 blocks
2 + 5 = 7 blocks

10. (3) $a = 12n$

Tina will earn a dollars if she sells n t-shirts at $12 each. Translating the sentence into an equation yields $a = 12n$.

11. (5) Not enough information is given.

Substitute a number from the x row in the table to find the corresponding y value in the row below. Because there is no x value provided for the missing y value, it is not possible to find y. Not enough information is given to solve the question.

12.

Substitute for r.

$t = \frac{72}{r} = 72 \div 6 = 12$

Skill 19 Algebraic Formulas
Pages 84–85

1. (4) 5

Choose the distance formula:
distance = rate × time
Solve for time.
time = distance ÷ rate
Substitute for distance and rate.
time = 1000 miles ÷ 200 mph = 5 hours

2. (5) 300(0.145)

Choose the simple interest rate formula:
interest = principal × rate × time
Convert 14.5% to a decimal:
14.5% ÷ 100 = 0.145
Substitute for the principal, the rate, and the time.
interest = $300 × 0.145 × 1 year
interest = $300(0.145)

3. (3) 8

Choose the total cost formula:
shipment cost = number of computers × price per computer
Solve for number of computers.
Number of computers = shipment cost ÷ price per computer
Substitute the known values from the row in the table that corresponds to shipment number 3.
Number of computers = $12,000 ÷ $1,500 = 8

4. (5) $7.20 ÷ 24

Linda bought 3 cases, but that does not affect the price per can. Choose the total cost formula:
total cost = (number of cans) × (price per can)
Solve for price per can.
Price per can = total cost ÷ number of cans
Substitute the known values into the formula.
Price per can = $7.20 ÷ 24

5. (2) 2 years

Choose the simple interest rate formula.
Solve for the time.
time = interest ÷ (principal × rate)
Convert the interest rate to a decimal:
6.25% ÷ 100 = 0.0625
Substitute the known values into the formula.
time = $625 ÷ ($5,000 × 0.0625)
time = $625 ÷ ($312.5) = 2

6.

Choose the distance formula.
Solve for rate.
rate = distance ÷ time
Substitute the known values into the formula.
Convert 90 minutes to hours: 90 minutes = 1.5 hours
rate = 150 miles ÷ 1.5 hours = 100 mph

7. (3) 7.4 mph

Choose the distance formula.
Solve for rate.
rate = distance ÷ time
Substitute the known values into the formula.
Choose the values that correspond to 5 miles.
Convert 41 minutes to hours:
41 minutes ÷ 60 minutes/hour = 0.68 hours
rate = 5 miles ÷ 0.68 hours = 7.4 mph

8. (3) between $2 and $3

Choose the total cost formula:
total cost = (number of gallons) × (cost per gallon)
Solve for cost per gallon.
cost per gallon = total cost ÷ number of gallons
Substitute the known values into the formula.
cost per gallon = $12.99 ÷ 5 = $2.60
$2.60 falls between $2 and $3.

9. (2) $12,000

Choose the simple interest rate formula.
Solve for the principal.
principal = interest ÷ (rate × time)
Convert the interest rate to a decimal:
$8\frac{1}{2}$% = 8.5% = 8.5 ÷ 100 = 0.085
Substitute the known values into the formula.
principal = $5100 ÷ (0.085 × 5 years)
principal = $5100 ÷ (0.425) = $12,000

10. (3) $1.29 ÷ 10

Choose the total cost formula:
total cost = (number of onions) × (price per onion)
Solve for price per onion.
price per onion = total cost ÷ number of onions
Substitute the known values into the formula.
price per onion = $1.29 ÷ 10

11. (2) distance formula

The question has variables for time, distance, and rate. These are the three variables that make up the distance formula: distance = rate × time.

12.

Choose the total cost formula:

total cost = (number of ounces) × (cost per ounce)

Solve for cost per ounce.

cost per ounce = total cost ÷ number of ounces

Substitute the known values into the formula.

cost per ounce = $12 ÷ 16 ounces = $0.75 per ounce

Skill 20 Algebra Word Problems
Pages 88–89

1. (3) 3n

Determine each quantity.

Hector's earnings 5 years ago = n

Hector's earnings today = $75,000

Set up an equation in words to represents the problem: three times Hector's earnings 5 years ago = Hector's earnings today.

$3n = \$75,000$

2. (4) 3

Determine each quantity.

Total movie tickets = 9

Child movie tickets = x

Adult movie tickets = $9 - x$

Total cost of movie tickets = $90

Set up an equation in words to represent the problem: $6 times the number of child tickets plus $12 times the number of adult tickets = $90.

$6x + 12(9 - x) = 90$

$6x + 108 - 12x = 90$

$-6x = -18$

$x = 3$ child tickets

3. (3) 4 m × 16 m

Determine each quantity.

width = x

length = $4x$

Set up an equation and solve:

length × width = 64 square meters

$x \times 4x = 64$

$4x^2 = 64$

$x^2 = 16$

$x = 4$

Substitute the value of x into the expressions for length and width.

width = $x = 4$

length = $4x = 4(4) = 16$

The dimensions are 4 m × 16 m.

4. (2) $x + x + 5 + x - 4 = 34$

Determine each quantity.

John's age = x

Alfredo's age = $x + 5$

Maria's age = $x - 4$

Set up an equation in words to represent the problem:

John's age + Alfredo's age + Maria's age = 34 years

Substitute into the word equation.

$x + x + 5 + x - 4 = 34$

5. (2) $178.60

Determine each quantity.

total cost = c

rental price per day = $29

price per mile over 100 miles = $0.60

mileage limit = 100

miles = 156

days = 5

Set up an equation in words to represent the problem: number of days × rental price per day + (the total miles driven − mileage limit) × price per mile over 100 miles = total cost

Substitute into the word equation.

$5(29) + (156 - 100)0.60 = c$

$145 + (56)0.60 = c$

$145 + 33.60 = c$

$\$178.60 = c$

6. (5) Not enough information is given.

Determine each quantity.

dog owners = x

cat owners = $2x$

total pet owners = y

Set up an equation in words:

dog owners + cat owners = total pet owners

Substitute the expressions into the word equation.

$x + 2x = y$

There are too many variables to solve this equation. To find the number of cat and dog owners, you need to know the total number of pet owners at the show.

7. (2) $\frac{30}{25}x$

Determine each quantity.

original money earned = x

original hours = 25

new money earned = y

new hours = 30

Set up an equation in words to represent the problem: new money earned ÷ new hours = original money earned ÷ original hours

Substitute the expressions into the word equation, and then solve for the new money earned, y.

$y \div 30 = x \div 25$

Multiply both sides by 30.

$y \div 30 \times 30 = x \div 25 \times 30$

$y = \frac{30}{25}x$

8. (2) $-5 - x$

Determine each quantity.

temperature at 9 A.M. = -5

temperature at 9 P.M. = x

temperature difference = y

Set up an equation in words to represents the problem:

temperature at 9 A.M. − temperature at 9 P.M. = temperature difference

Substitute and then solve for the temperature difference, y.

$-5 - x = y$

9.

Determine each quantity.

one number $= x$

larger number $= x + 4$

sum of the numbers $= 18$

Set up an equation in words to represents the problem: one number + larger number = sum

Substitute the expressions into the word equation, and then solve.

$x + x + 4 = 18$

$2x + 4 = 18$

$2x = 14$

$x = 7$

Substitute x into the expression for the larger number.

larger number $= x + 4 = 7 + 4 = 11$

10. **(3) 23**

Determine each quantity.

Mr. Pearce's students $= x$

Ms. Felder's students $= x + 6$

total students $= 40$

Set up an equation in words to represents the problem: Mr. Pearce's students + Ms. Felder's students = total students

Substitute and then solve.

$x + x + 6 = 40$

$2x + 6 = 40$

$2x = 34$

$x = 17$

Substitute x into the expression to find the number of students Ms. Felder has.

Ms. Felder's students $= x + 6 = 17 + 6 = 23$

11. **(4) $p - \$1.50 - \$3.00$**

Choose a variable to represent one quantity, then write expressions to represent the other quantities.

clock price $= p$

coupon $= \$1.50$

rebate $= \$3.00$

total price $= y$

Set up an equation in words to represents the problem.

clock price − coupon − rebate = total price

Substitute the expressions into the word equation, then solve.

$p - \$1.50 - \$3.00 = y$

12. **(4) $2z + 2(z + 7) = 54$**

width $= z$

length $= z + 7$

perimeter $= 54$ inches

Set up an equation in words to represent the problem:

2 widths + 2 lengths = perimeter

Substitute and then solve.

$2z + 2(z + 7) = 54$

[Pretest Answer Sheet: Mathematics]

Name: _____ Class: _____ Date: _____

1 ①②③④⑤	**5** ①②③④⑤	**9** ①②③④⑤	**13** ①②③④⑤	**17** ①②③④⑤
2 ①②③④⑤	**6** ①②③④⑤	**10** ①②③④⑤	**14** ①②③④⑤	**18** ①②③④⑤
3 ①②③④⑤	**7** ①②③④⑤	**11** ①②③④⑤	**15** ①②③④⑤	**19** ①②③④⑤
4 ①②③④⑤	**8** ①②③④⑤	**12** ①②③④⑤	**16** ①②③④⑤	**20** ①②③④⑤

© 2009 Steck-Vaughn, an imprint of HMH Supplemental Publishers Inc. Permission granted to reproduce for classroom use.

Pretest Answer Sheet   **127**

Name: _____ Class: _____ Date: _____

Time Started: _____

Time Finished: _____

Part I

1 ①②③④⑤

2 ①②③④⑤

3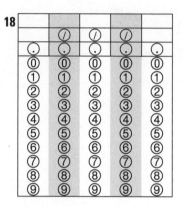

4

5 ①②③④⑤

6 ①②③④⑤

7 ①②③④⑤

8 ①②③④⑤

9 ①②③④⑤

10

11 ①②③④⑤

12 ①②③④⑤

13 ①②③④⑤

END OF PART I

You must stop using your calculator now.

Part II

14 ①②③④⑤

15 ①②③④⑤

16 ①②③④⑤

17 ①②③④⑤

18

19 ①②③④⑤

20 ①②③④⑤

21 ①②③④⑤

22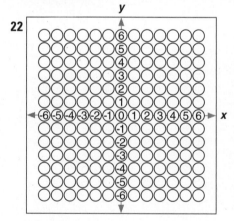

23 ①②③④⑤

24 ①②③④⑤

25 ①②③④⑤